W9-BHB-722

REAL JUSTICE:

GUILTY OF
BEING WEIRD

• • •

THE STORY OF GUY PAUL MORIN

CYNTHIA J. FARYON

LORIMER

JAMES LORIMER & COMPANY LTD., PUBLISHERS
TORONTO

James Lorimer & Company Ltd., Publishers acknowledges the support of the Ontario Arts Council. We acknowledge the financial support of the Government of Canada through the Canada Book Fund for our publishing activities. We acknowledge the support of the Canada Council for the Arts which last year invested $24.3 million in writing and publishing throughout Canada. We acknowledge the Government of Ontario through the Ontario Media Development Corporation's Ontario Book Initiative.

Canada Council
for the Arts

ONTARIO ARTS COUNCIL
CONSEIL DES ARTS DE L'ONTARIO

Library and Archives Canada Cataloguing in Publication

Faryon, Cynthia J., 1956-
     Real justice : guilty of being weird : the story of Guy
Paul Morin / Cynthia J. Faryon.

(Real justice)
Includes bibliographical references and index.
Also issued in electronic format.
ISBN 978-1-4594-0092-4 (pbk.).--ISBN 978-1-4594-0093-1 (bound)

     1. Morin, Guy Paul--Juvenile literature. 2. Murder--Ontario--
Queensville--Juvenile literature. 3. Judicial error--Canada--Juvenile
literature. 4. False imprisonment--Canada--Juvenile literature.
I. Title. II. Title: Guilty of being weird.

HV6535.C33Q84 2012   j364.15'23092   C2012-903724-9

James Lorimer & Company Ltd.,   Distributed in the United States by:
Publishers   Orca Book Publishers
317 Adelaide Street West, Suite 1002   P.O. Box 468
Toronto, ON, Canada   Custer, WA, USA
M5V 1P9   98240-0468
www.lorimer.ca

Printed and bound in Canada.
Manufactured by Friesens Corporation in Altona, Manitoba, Canada in August 2012.
Job #77087

FOR LISE AND LEON

"The justice system failed me, but science saved me. My lawyers did the best they could through the avenues of the justice system. But in the end, science gave the final word. Science is wonderful. I love science."

— Guy Paul Morin

CONTENTS

NOTE

Throughout this book, the author has endeavoured to use quoted dialogue. The sources include: newspaper articles, trial transcripts, Inquiry reports and witness statements, police reports, and public documents, as well as other publications. When quoted dialogue is not available, a limited amount of reconstructed or constructed conversation has been created from the facts of the case, the evidence and reports, and the likelihood of the dialogue, in order to help explain or highlight the facts of the story.

FOREWORD

It is shocking to think that as recently as thirty years ago, most Canadian citizens believed that anyone imprisoned for a crime was probably guilty. For reasons that now seem naïve, it was assumed that the justice system always reached a correct result; that the wisdom of twelve jurors always resulted in the right people being sent to prison. In fact, verdicts were so unquestioned that the phrase "wrongful conviction" had yet to be coined.

The first case to shake that belief was Donald Marshall Jr., an aboriginal street person who was *exonerated* of murder only after he had endured eleven years behind bars. The justice system was embarrassed by the Marshall debacle. The public was taken aback. However, the Marshall case was seen as an anomaly: a one-time mistake caused by a unique set of factors.

It took the case of Guy Paul Morin to jolt the country

into an awareness of just how vulnerable the court system could be. Where Marshall's *conviction* had been of little interest to his community in Halifax, Morin's arrest and trial received full coverage by the central Canadian media. Top defence lawyers at both his original trial and his retrial argued fiercely that Morin was innocent of the abduction and murder of Christine Jessop. The evidence in his case was examined and re-examined with a fine-tooth comb. Witnesses were grilled for days on end. Yet, the system failed and Mr. Morin came close to spending the rest of his days in Kingston Penitentiary for a crime he didn't commit.

How could it happen? Many reasons lie behind Morin's 1992 conviction, beginning with the fact that he struck people as a strange, eccentric young man. When a murder investigation gets underway, bad luck for anyone who does not fit within society's idea of "normal," because fingers will immediately begin pointing at them.

As the prosecution unravelled, "foolproof" evidence was found to be badly flawed. Evidence which had been concealed from Morin's lawyers turned out to be very important in determining whether he had, or had not, murdered Christine. Human error led to mistakes in processing evidence, and inexperienced police work resulted in blind spots in the investigation.

A number of unusual features mark the Morin case, making it one that deserves to be studied closely for decades to come.

For example, the proximity of the Morin and Jessop families — next-door neighbours whose differences heated up into an outright feud — was unique and fateful. A justice system that had only begun to come to grips with the role of victims allowed the Jessop family to help steer the course of the investigation in questionable ways. And the strained relationship between the families clearly fired up suspicion against the Morins. To the Jessops, the police, and the community, the Morins were seen as caricatures: a breed of sub-humans capable of anything.

Another unusual feature was that the Morin case became one of very few instances where a not-guilty verdict in a murder case was overturned and a new trial was ordered. It also became the first trial where DNA evidence played a key role in proving someone's innocence.

After the Morin case, the message for the Canadian legal system is: If Guy Paul Morin could be found guilty — in front of the national media and after a nine-month trial fought by highly skilled lawyers — how many more past convictions may have been wrong? How many times will it happen again?

We have some partial answers. In the years since Morin left prison and disappeared into a normal life, there have been almost two dozen high-profile exonerations in homicide cases. It's a terrible toll that shows the weaknesses of a justice system that places too much emphasis on bad science, eager eyewitnesses, and police who can distort evidence if they assume they have the right suspect.

Guy Paul Morin was nothing more than a slightly odd individual who lived on the wrong street at the wrong time. However, the lessons of his case will long outlive Morin himself, providing an example of how seriously justice can go off the rails.

— Kirk Makin
Crime reporter for *The Globe and Mail*
and author of *Redrum the Innocent*

1

CHAPTER ONE

CRIES IN THE NIGHT

OCTOBER 5, 1984: SUNDERLAND, ON,
IN DURHAM REGION, 56 KM FROM THE
TOWN OF QUEENSVILLE

"Help!" Lydia Robertson jumped awake. Her bedroom
was dark. Did she hear that scream or was she dreaming?
She lay there quietly for a moment and listened.

"Help!" She hadn't dreamt it. A girl screamed for help.

Leaving the lights off, she slipped out of bed and
crept down the stairs to the front door to peer out. A
gust of chilly October wind poured over her from the
open door and she shivered. It was too dark to see anything; there were no street lights out in the country, just a
moon and stars. A neighbour's dog barked. Leaves rustled
in the wind. Faintly she heard the slam of a car door and
the sound of a child crying, then silence. *It was probably
one of the neighbours arguing*, she thought to herself. *It was*

none of her business. She shut the door and went back upstairs to bed.

She wasn't the only neighbour on Ravenshoe Road who was startled awake. Another neighbour across the road was also disturbed from her sleep by the sounds that night. "Help . . . don't . . . please!"

Lydia's neighbour shook her husband awake. "Someone is screaming *help*, I heard it," she said, and they both lay there quietly listening. Minutes dragged by: nothing.

"You're dreaming," the man said to his wife as he rolled over and went back to sleep.

A third neighbour sat up in bed. He heard his dogs barking, but thought he had also heard a girl screaming. He listened quietly, then heard the sound of a car door slamming and relaxed. *Just the teenager across the road getting home late,* he thought to himself.

2

CHAPTER TWO

GUY PAUL AND THE MORIN FAMILY

SEPTEMBER 1984 (A MONTH EARLIER):
QUEENSVILLE, ON, IN YORK REGION,
22 KM NORTH OF TORONTO

The York Region police cruiser slowed to a stop in front of the Morin house — again. They didn't have to look at the address to find the place. They knew which house it was by the floodlights invading the night sky, and the noise of saws and hammers assaulting the quiet of the country road.

"Mr. Morin," one of them called out after entering the yard littered with old cars, a cement mixer, lumber, and numerous tools. "Mr. Morin!"

Alphonse (Al) Morin looked up, saw the police, and sighed. He flipped the off switch on the table saw alongside the house. His son, Guy Paul, turned to see why his dad had killed the saw and also sighed at the sight of the officers in the yard. He stopped hammering and climbed down the ladder.

"Don't you people have something better to do than bother us? This is our house and our yard. We're not robbing or stealing. We're trying to renovate our home here. Tell our neighbours to leave us alone, eh?" said Al.

"Mr. Morin, it is late, and people are trying to sleep. You'll have to shut it down for the night."

"I don't see the police knocking on the Jessops' door when Kenny is pounding on those drums of his. Only us, you come bothering," said Guy Paul. "Those people across the road are always calling the cops on us. They've even made complaints to the town council, trying to get an order against us. Don't you think it's weird that they are the only ones complaining while the Jessops, who live right next door, never say a thing about the noise?"

"Well, they have a right to sleep, just as you have a right to fix up your house. Shut it down after dark, and then they'll probably stop complaining."

"It's not just the noise; they complain about everything. Those people complain about my bees, say they're a menace, and about our dogs, Jessie and James. Dogs bark sometimes. They're dogs. And they don't like how our yard looks with the old cars I'm fixing up. They have no business. No business at all, telling us how to live," said Guy Paul.

At the end of it all, the police got into their cruiser and drove away. Ida, Guy Paul's mother, came out of the house and while the men shut down for the night, a very loud anti-neighbour discussion took place. When the door shut behind them, everyone in the cluster of four houses along the Queensville cemetery knew exactly how the Morins felt about their neighbours.

• • •

In the 1980s, boys dreamed of fast muscle cars — Mustangs, Chargers, Camaros, Firebirds — with wide tires, spoilers, and metallic paint. Even a geeky, shy boy with a face splotched with acne got the hot girl, as long as he had the hot car. After school on Fridays teenagers parked them in their driveways and washed the cars until they shone.

Twenty-four-year-old Guy Paul Morin was one of six kids, but the only one still living at home. He loved cars and enjoyed seeing the muscle cars roaring down the hillside. He, however, didn't own a muscle car. He drove his parents' Honda with gold-coloured seat covers. He seldom washed it and never vacuumed it. He was considered by his peers to be boring and somewhat of a nerd. He kept bees and grew flowers to encourage the hives behind his house. Like many twenty-four-year-olds, he was heavily into music. He loved it so much he played two instruments and was a member of three bands. Only he didn't play the drums or electric guitar: he played saxophone and clarinet and he loved the music of the 1940s.

Guy Paul liked girls his age and had casually dated a few over the years. But he was a geek without a hot car, so he never got to date the hot girls. He kept busy helping his father renovate the family home, looking after his bees, and tinkering on the beat-up cars littering the yard. He didn't smoke cigarettes or pot. He didn't drink or go to parties. His hair was short and well kept, yet due to his employment as a labourer he dressed sloppily. After graduating from high school he took courses in air conditioning and refrigeration, auto upholstery, spray painting, and gas fitting. In July 1984, he started work with Interiors International Limited, a furniture manufacturing company, as a finishing sander. He loved working nights, but his boss had recently scheduled him for the day shift, so he decided he would quit when November came.

Guy Paul's father, Alphonse Morin, was a retired teacher from Seneca College who had served with the Royal Military Engineers during the Second World War. His family was French-Canadian and his father was domineering. Growing up in semi-seclusion on the prairies, Alphonse had enjoyed the wide open spaces and the privacy that went with farm living. The trouble was, he didn't live on the farm anymore and he had neighbours who had their own ideas about peace and quiet.

Al and Guy Paul often argued about how to go about the renovations on their home. Sometimes Ida would get into the middle of the argument and all the neighbours would hear the yelling, name calling, and sometimes slamming of doors. Often the police were called to make sure it wasn't violent. It never was. They were simply expressive.

Ida was English-born and was raised in Bermuda before immigrating to Canada. After marrying Alphonse and settling down to raise a family, she became a stay-at-home mom and worked part-time as a volunteer and substitute teacher.

Most of the residents of Queensville had heard about the neighbour problems. Feeling bullied, the Morins didn't join in community functions or school gatherings. Their absence fuelled the town gossip.

"The Morins have six children: Lisette, Yvette, Diane, Raymond, Denise, and Guy Paul, who is the only one living at home. At his age, if you can imagine! Guy Paul is a weird type of guy," the Jessops were told by the previous owners of their house. "Most people in Queensville think the whole family is weird. Guy Paul is a clarinet player and is always in his room alone, playing and staring out of the window. It's creepy, him looking into our yard all the time. I'm sure he's harmless, just weird."

So when the Jessops moved into their home in 1983, they were at first leery of the Morins until Ida and Al came over with a casserole to welcome them to the neighbourhood. While the two families were never friends, they were friendly neighbours. Robert Jessop often talked to Al about his home projects and borrowed tools, and Ida brought them fresh vegetables from her garden. In September of 1984, Guy Paul went to the Jessops' to light the pilot light for their hot water tank. He also gave them honey from his hives and tried to talk to Kenny about music, which didn't go over very well. Their music was generations apart. When Janet was going to be late getting home from her part-time job, she often asked Al and Ida to watch the kids until she got home. The Morins were happy to find the Jessops so easy to get along with and the Jessops were glad the Morins were so private. When Robert Jessop went to jail for fraud, Janet told everyone he was working in California and the Morins never asked any questions.

Al and Ida often wondered why Janet hadn't asked them to watch her daughter the day Christine went missing.

3

CHAPTER THREE

THE DAY CHRISTINE WENT MISSING, PART ONE

OCTOBER 3, 1984: GUY PAUL MORIN

It seemed like any other Wednesday for Guy Paul Morin. He was up early to get ready for work. His mother was getting ready for her part-time teaching job, but Al was still in bed. She put Guy Paul's breakfast on the table and poured him a glass of juice.

"I made a grocery list for you," Ida said. "Just a few things we need. Don't forget to check the specials."

"Always do," he said.

Guy Paul put his dishes in the sink before he left the house and let the dogs out into the yard. He also checked his hives before leaving for work. This weekend he was moving them out to his parents' other property off Ravenshoe Road. The neighbours had increased their "bee" complaints, so he'd told his dad he'd move them. Secretly he was glad to move them. The noise from the renovations upset the bees; the peace and quiet in the country would be good for them.

Guy Paul drove to work in Newmarket, about forty minutes away. He put his things in his locker in the lunch room. Some of the guys were getting ready and laughing and talking about girls and parties and getting drunk. The radio was blaring in the shop — rock and roll, screaming guitars — and the sound of tools made his head hurt. He punched his time card, then went to his work area.

He really missed working the night shift. It was so quiet; he didn't have to talk to anyone. He could turn the radio to CBC and think and enjoy what he was doing. On days, he was stuck working with men who smoked and talked about how badly they were hungover. Guy Paul had nothing in common with them. They pried into his life, asked questions, and made fun of him. Why couldn't people just let him be?

After his shift, Guy Paul punched out his time card at 3:32 p.m. On the way home he parked the car on the second-level parking lot at the Upper Canada Mall in Newmarket and went downstairs to the Infoplace ticket kiosk, as he did every Wednesday.

"Hello, Guy Paul," said the sales girl. "Your usual?"

She was pretty and Guy Paul liked her. She was the only reason why he bought his tickets at the mall.

"Yes, please. Wouldn't it be great if this one's a winner?"

"It could happen," she said.

"See you next week."

As he did every week, he neatly folded his ticket in half and slipped it into his wallet. He then took the escalator up to the Dominion store and bought the items on his mother's list. He filled up with gas across from the mall and stopped at Loblaw's, on the other side of the intersection, and then drove to Mr. Grocers. He pulled to a stop in front of the doors and read the specials posted on the windows, as he did every Wednesday. There was nothing they needed, so he didn't go in.

Guy Paul arrived at home between 5:30 and 6:00 p.m. His brother-in-law, Frank Devine, was leaving and they stood and talked in the driveway for a couple of minutes while the dogs bounced around barking. After putting the bags of groceries in the kitchen, he went into the living room to say hi to his mother and his sister.

"Do the Jessops have company?" his sister Yvette asked.

"Don't know, why?" said Guy Paul.

"There was a different car in the driveway a few minutes after the school bus drove off. Maybe they got a new car."

"No clue," he said. "Their car was there when I pulled in."

Guy Paul left his sister and mother in the living room and went to his parents' bedroom to take a nap. His mother woke him at 6:30 and they ate around 7 p.m. His sister had already left.

After supper, Guy Paul and Al went outside, set up floodlights, and started work. They dug a new drainage trench and poured cement before starting on the insulation. Al was in and out of the house while they worked, so only Guy Paul saw the police cruiser pull into the Jessops' driveway shortly after 8 p.m.

"Mom, Dad," he yelled as he went into the house. "Cops are here again. Damn neighbours probably complained." They looked at each other and rolled their eyes. It wasn't even late yet.

"They aren't coming here," said Ida, looking out the window. "They're going next door to the Jessops'."

Guy Paul and his father went outside to take a closer look.

"Hey, something must be going on, eh?" said Guy Paul to his father.

"Probably not, maybe another complaint," said Al.

"Something must be going on," said Guy Paul when the second cruiser pulled up. "I . . . I'm really good when it comes to predictions; I bet that little Christine is gone."

"Christine, do you think?" said Al. "Nah, maybe Ken, something else maybe. You know, Ken's at the age, you know, just socializing. Maybe Ken's at that age when he's starting to get into trouble, eh?"

Ken and the officer came over to the fence and said: "Did you see Christine?"

"No, not all day," said Al. "Why?"

"Her mother has reported her missing. We're looking for her."

"Holy shit, Dad, I was right," said Guy Paul after the police officer left.

4

CHAPTER FOUR

THE DAY CHRISTINE WENT MISSING, PART TWO

OCTOBER 3, 1984: CHRISTINE JESSOP

"Skeeter-Deeter," Janet Jessop said to her nine-year-old daughter, Christine. "I'm going to see Dad today and then I'm taking Kenny to the dentist. We might be home by four, but we might not, too. Do your chores when you get home and if you go anywhere leave me a message, so I know where you are."

"Sure." Christine answered, sticking her tongue out at her fourteen-year-old brother Kenny, then grinning impishly.

Nine-year-old Christine Marion Jessop (Chrissy) was always "happy, sensitive, lively, caring, and a little clean-freak," said Janet Jessop years later. "And she was the little type [physically]. She could go from a real lady to a little tomboy. Her brother, maybe, thought she was a pain in the neck, but she would always say, 'Mind your own business, Kenny,' or 'Get away from me,' just like that."

Christine had an ordinary day at school, with one exception. She and the other kids in her class had each been given a recorder, a musical instrument, to take home. Christine couldn't wait to show it to everyone. She got off the school bus at about five minutes to four. She waved at the paperboy, picked up the newspaper and the mail, and brought it with her into the house. She left everything on the counter in the kitchen except for the recorder. She grabbed a nickel and rode her bike to the store.

"Hi, Christine. What's that you got there?" said the store owner.

"It's a recorder from school. I'm going to learn to play. The teacher taught us to play 'Three Blind Mice' . . . Can I have some bubble gum?" He gave it to her and gave her the change.

"Have a good afternoon," he said.

"Yup," she said as she walked outside.

A few minutes later, a passerby saw Christine standing across from the store holding a bag of candy in one hand and her recorder in the other. She was standing with two small boys about her age and a boy of about eleven or twelve who seemed to be explaining something to the others. She appeared to be waiting for someone or something. The passerby was later told by police that it was a girl, not an older boy he'd seen; however, the witness always maintained Christine was with a boy.

The next conversation Christine had was with the person who murdered her.

• • •

The afternoon Christine went missing, Janet picked up her son, Kenny, from school. They went to visit Robert Jessop at the Toronto East Detention Centre. After the visit, Janet dropped Kenny off for his dentist appointment in the nearby town of Newmarket and did some errands. She arrived back at the dentist, paid their bill, and at about 4 p.m. they drove home.

The house looked quiet when Janet and Ken arrived home. Janet pulled the car to a stop in front of the shed leading to the back door. Christine's bike was lying on its side in the shed. The pink sweater she had worn to school that morning was hanging on a nail high on the shed wall. It was too high for Christine to reach, which Janet thought was a bit strange. What really concerned her was the kickstand on her daughter's bike was bent.

"Chrissy," Janet called as they walked into the house. There was no answer and her jacket wasn't on her peg next to the door. The family dog, Freckles, was sitting in the corner of the kitchen.

"She's not home, Ma," said Kenny.

"Her school bag is on the counter, so she's been home," Janet said. "Kenny, was Chrissy's kickstand on her bike bent before?"

"I dunno, don't think so." Kenny checked downstairs, thinking she might be with her pet frog, but the basement was empty.

"Chrissy! Answer me!" Janet called again, again no answer. She found it a bit strange that Christine hadn't left a note, but figured she would come bursting through the door soon. Janet made herself a cup of coffee then called her husband's lawyer. When she hung up, Christine was still missing.

"In those days, I thought you shouldn't call the police until you'd at least looked around a bit. So I drove to the park to see if she was there. There was no sign of her. I just got that feeling in the pit of my stomach. We looked everywhere for her. I phoned all her friends."

No one had seen Christine since the school bus had dropped her off.

Kenny went to the cemetery to see if she was playing there. Christine liked playing hide-and-seek among the gravestones and sometimes she took the flowers off the graves and brought them home. One summer she'd set up a stand at the end of the drive and sold the cemetery flowers to people driving by.

She wasn't in the cemetery. Janet was mystified, annoyed, and starting to get scared. Christine should have waited for them to get home. She shouldn't have run off to play without leaving a note or phone number or something. Janet told Kenny she'd be right back and went to check the cemetery herself. It would be just like Christine to hide on her brother and Janet wasn't in the playing mood.

"Christine!" she called. "Christine, answer me."

The headstones were casting their shadows in the fading light. In the valley below, lights were starting to shine from the farmhouse windows. The October breeze had a chill to it. Janet was really scared now. There was no sign of Christine. She didn't want to panic, but hurried back into the house.

"I knew then something had to be wrong, and so we picked up the phone and called the police."

5

CHAPTER FIVE

THE SEARCH BEGINS

OCTOBER 3, 1984

Constables McGowan and Bunce of the York Regional Police department arrived shortly before 8 p.m. The constables and Janet were sitting at the kitchen table and Kenny was hovering close by.

"We were home at four-ten and Christine was nowhere to be seen," Janet told them.

"How do you know what time it was?" asked the officer.

"I have a new watch ... see?" Kenny held up his wrist.

"I looked at the kitchen wall clock because I had promised my husband I would call his lawyer and give him a message. I knew when I came in, I had time to have a cup of coffee before I had to call him. His office closes at five."

"Were there any family problems, or problems at

school, or with friends? Was she upset today, or acting a bit strange?" asked Constable Bunce.

"No, none. Christine is happy, she loves life, her family, school, and sports. We've never had problems with her and she's never been missing before. This isn't like her to do this."

"Where does she spend her time after school and on weekends?"

"She loves her bike. Rides it down to the park to play with her friends or watch ball games. She plays in the cemetery sometimes. If she goes to a friend's house she calls me to let me know where she is. She never talks to people she doesn't know," said Janet.

"Were you in a hurry to get home because you knew Christine was here?" asked the constable.

"Yes. That's how I know when we got home. I kept looking at the time and hurrying to get home for when she got home from school."

"Did you see any cars parked in front of your house when you were coming up Leslie Street?" he asked.

"No," said Janet, "I honestly didn't notice."

Queensville was a small town of about 630; everyone knew everyone else. It had its share of missing person cases over the years, but they were children who had been lost or were runaways. The York Regional police

decided this was just another one. Their first concern was
that the young girl would be exposed to the October
weather overnight, if she wasn't found. They also were
concerned she might be hurt and couldn't get home. A
kidnapping was not seriously considered. It was a very
small community, and it would be tough for someone to
kidnap a child without witnesses.

Over the next seven hours there were thirteen police
cars, two emergency vehicles, and seventeen police
officers at the Jessops', including a large truck with spot-
lights on top. A missing child was a huge undertaking
for the small and understaffed police department. They
were used to noisy neighbour complaints, nothing serious enough to make demands on the very small police
department. Cell phones, computers, *Amber Alert* systems:
none of these options were open to the police in 1984.
Note taking, tape recorders, outdated filing systems, and
old-fashioned leg work were all they had.

"I know you said you called everyone, Mrs. Jessop,"
the police told her. "Call them all again and anyone else
that comes to mind, like relatives. Ask them if they've
seen her, or spoken to her, or if she is or was over at their
house today."

No one had seen Christine, but because of the calls,
people started to arrive at the house to see if they could

help. Soon the place was filled with people. They made coffee and tea, and helped themselves to drinks from the refrigerator. They touched glasses, mugs, counter tops, and door handles, and used the bathroom. Someone picked up the bike from off the shed floor and leaned it against the wall. Perhaps the same person also took Christine's pink sweater off the nail and brought it into the house, most likely thinking they were helping. The police didn't monitor who was coming into the house or what they were doing. They hadn't taped off Christine's bedroom or the shed, or treated the house like a crime scene. They treated the situation as if Christine was staying too long at a friend's house, or maybe she was lost in the woods. The police didn't even speak to most of them. Why go to all that trouble when it wasn't necessary?

So, the family, friends, and neighbours were all free to come and go, perhaps smudging the kidnapper's fingerprints, palm prints, dirty foot prints, or even the signs of a struggle. The killer himself may have come back to the house, showed sympathy to Janet and Ken, or even helped with the search. No one would ever know how much evidence was destroyed in that first seven hours.

"Perhaps you didn't want to admit it to yourself that Christine … was in some very serious trouble," Inspector Tony Wilson told the Commission years later.

The police failed to do a house-to-house search, choosing instead to only knock on the doors of the houses closest to the Jessops'. Other homes were visited randomly by searchers without notes taken on who was in the house they canvassed or what they said.

"Why aren't they fingerprinting?" one of the visitors at the Jessops' asked her husband. "Why are they letting all these people go around touching things? Constable Bunce," she then called out. "My husband and I would like to have a word with you."

"Certainly, Ma'am, Sir."

"When we arrived," the man said. "Janet called out 'Come in. Christine's gone missing,' with almost as much emotion as if she had given me the baseball scores."

"That's right, Constable," said his wife. "She was sitting at the table drinking coffee. She was very quiet. I guess she was in shock, but it's kind of bizarre. She is calm, as if nothing has happened. I would think she'd be looking around the house, trying to figure out where her daughter is. Strange."

"Could it be that she's just one of those people who conceals their emotions? Have you ever seen her upset before?" the constable asked.

"When Janet's mother died, she was so upset she had to take Valium to calm herself. Yet with her daughter missing, she seems completely relaxed. She says Christine is safe and warm and will be home soon."

Strange, thought the officer. *I wonder if she knows something we don't.*

Constable McGowan went to the Morin household to see if they had seen the little girl.

"Maybe you're aware the little girl next door never came home today," he said. "We're looking all over the neighbourhood and we'd appreciate it if we could come in and do a quick search of your house. Just in case Christine is hiding somewhere."

"You don't need to do that," Alphonse interrupted him. "We already had a good look around. We don't need anybody else searching in here. She's not here."

"Are you saying we can't come in, Mr. Morin?"

"That's right. But I'll look again around the house after you leave. You can look around the yard and shed if you want."

Guy Paul was sitting close by, listening, but didn't say a word; he sat quietly and stared straight in front of him. The officer felt it was an odd reaction, considering the little girl that lived right next door to him was lost. The officer went to the Morin backyard to look at the ditch where they had poured cement. Al followed him.

"Now don't try and come up the stairs. They're under

construction and we don't want any lawsuits if you get hurt."

An identification officer arrived around midnight to fingerprint the bicycle and take pictures. Since no one had been fingerprinted, the prints taken from the bike were useless. There was no record of who was in or out of the house, or who touched the bike. They hadn't even taken fingerprints from Christine's room. There was no way of knowing whose fingerprints were supposed to be there and whose weren't.

At about 1 a.m. on October 4, two police officers returned with a dog named Ryder and asked permission to search the Morin property again. (Ryder was not a police dog; he was a personal pet belonging to Constable Robertson's family. Robertson had been training the dog for police work and felt Ryder may be able to sniff out the little girl.) Al agreed and called his dogs indoors.

"Mr. Morin," one of the officers said to Guy Paul, "have you seen Christine Jessop since she got off the school bus yesterday afternoon?"

"Nope," said Guy Paul, "I didn't see her at all. When I arrived home from work around five-thirty, six, the Jessops' car was in the driveway."

Robertson made detailed notes of his dog-search, listing the buildings, vehicles, bushes, and swamps he and his dog went to. He made notes on who was interviewed, but never mentioned the dog's reaction to the Morins or their property.

A mobile home was set up at the fire hall as a command post. Phone lines and typewriters were set up so the police could be continually updated on the search efforts. A map of Queensville showing the search areas was hung on the wall, highlighting farmers' fields, ponds, and ditches. When an area was searched it was crossed off the map. There was no list of who was involved in the search, or which individuals searched which area. None of the searchers were told to report anything suspicious or look for articles of clothing. They were only instructed to search for the little girl who was lost or could be laying hurt somewhere.

"Have you seen her at all, Mr. Lewis?" a farm owner was asked by a young boy waving Christine's picture. "She never came home today."

"No, young man. I haven't seen her, don't think I've ever seen her," he replied.

"I helped with the search," Mr. Lewis said years later. "I searched the barns and the fields that night, and four more times in the days afterward. Every time I turned over a bale of hay, I was afraid she would be underneath. I'd have crapped my pants."

A small group of townspeople were searching the ditches alongside a farmer's field when a silver car pulled up. A blond man, in his early twenties, got out of the car and asked what they were doing. They told him about Christine and he offered to help them look. No one would have remembered him at all except he asked a lot of questions about the search areas and hid when a police cruiser passed by. No one wrote down the make of his car, or the licence plate number.

As the hours passed, the police began to think this was more than a straightforward case of a lost child. Since Janet seemed so calm, they wondered if she and her husband had planned this as a ruse in order to gain an early release for Robert. They confronted her and warned her that if they found out she was involved, they would charge her with public mischief. Janet simply stared at them.

The search was officially called off on the weekend of October 7. No one had found a trace of Christine.

"After the search," said Detective Nechay years later, "we knew that something had happened. She wasn't in the general area of Queensville, so we looked at it more seriously and then, honestly, in the back of our minds we knew that something had happened, but what we didn't know."

Christine Jessop had simply vanished.

6

CHAPTER SIX

THE TRAIL

OCTOBER 4, 1984

The police begged for leads in the newspapers and on television. Telephone poles, stores, the back windows of cars: all had posters of the missing child. Missing, they all said. They all asked for information. And from these white pages, the sparkling eyes, impish grin, and innocent expression of Christine tore at the heartstrings. The public response was overwhelming. The police response to the flood of calls, however, was disorganized.

"York Regional Police Service, can I help you?"

"I'm not sure," said Mrs. Horwood into the phone. "It's about that little girl who went missing. It could be nothing, but my husband and I saw something strange the day she disappeared."

"Do you mean the Jessop girl, Ma'am?" asked the desk sergeant.

"Yes. We were stopped at the intersection in town, and we saw this male driver in a very dirty, dark green or blue, 1979 two-door Buick on Queensville Sideroad on October 3, 1984, at about 4:05 p.m. He was slouched down in his seat and seemed to be holding down a child with long, dark hair in a very forceful manner close to his chest with his right arm. We followed this Buick north on Leslie Street. The car turned west onto Fieldstone Lane in the Balmoral Heights subdivision. It drove up this street very slowly and close to the curb. We couldn't turn to follow him right away because of traffic, so he drove out of sight. But, well, we were so concerned that we followed it into the subdivision and drove slowly around the block looking for the car. But we lost it."

"If you can please give me your name, address, and phone number, an officer will contact you further."

This tip was put in a file to be followed up on and by the end of the day was buried under a stack of other reports made by concerned citizens. The caller wasn't contacted for nearly two weeks. No one at the police department contacted motor vehicle branch for information on a vehicle matching the description. No one canvassed the residents in the Balmoral Heights subdivision to see if anyone living there had a car like the one reported, or knew anyone with such a car.

"Hello, is this an officer?" A local woman who claimed to have psychic powers called the York Police. "I had a dream last evening, Officer," she said. "It was Christine. She told me she drowned and her body is lying in a nearby marsh."

Arrangements were made and the psychic led the officers to a field, next to a marsh. Dogs were brought in, and a team of men in hip-waders searched the area. Nothing was found.

Another psychic called and told the officer: "I was told in a vision she has fallen into an old well." Officers contacted a local man to help search a field with a divining rod. Nothing was found.

Another psychic told Janet that her daughter was close by and being cared for. Janet was thrilled, and so relieved, but the psychic couldn't tell anyone where she was. This tip was taken seriously and officers canvassed the neighbourhood but turned up nothing.

Another caller said she had noticed a strange young man in the area of Sharon and Newmarket the day Christine went missing. Shortly after she heard about Christine's disappearance, she saw him cleaning his van. A few days later, and before the police had a chance to question him, the man disappeared.

Guy Paul Morin's sister, Yvette Devine, called the

police and told them about the white car in the Jessop driveway the day Christine went missing. She couldn't remember much about it. She went under hypnosis to see if she could remember a licence plate but couldn't.

A number of suspects were "looked into" during the weeks that followed, but all were dismissed for having *alibis* or for passing a lie-detector test. Some very strong leads were never followed up on at all. The police never made a list of residents, visitors, or out-of-town workers in the area during the time Christine went missing. Many of the notes and reports that were taken disappeared.

The residents of Queensville were quiet in the days, weeks, and months that followed. Small children were kept close — very close. No one officially used the word "kidnapped," but most were thinking it. The only ones who knew for sure were the kidnapper and Christine Jessop.

Halloween came and went; the dark streets were almost empty of trick-or-treaters. Parents guided their children, holding tightly on to their hands. No child played at the park alone. None rode their bikes through the streets, or stopped at the store for bubble gum, or wandered to and from houses in the small neighbourhoods.

"Oh, there's some scared people here. I walk my son to school and back every day. And the neighbours do the same thing," said a local resident.

The officers drove the route Janet and Kenny took on the day Christine went missing, to verify the timing. The investigators were convinced that if Janet and Robert Jessop weren't directly involved with Christine's disappearance, a neighbour or a friend of the family was. They even interviewed the previous owner of the Jessop house. The officer was told:

"Guy Paul acts weird. If you want more details," she said, "talk to the second house north of the Jessops' and these people will tell you lots. He's never worked and is always home."

Guy Paul under arrest for Christine's murder

School photo of Christine Jessop, age nine

Christine's body was found just off the large bend in the path

The Jessop house as seen from the Morins' backyard

The Morin home as seen from the Jessops' driveway

Guy Paul exiting prison on bail

7

CHAPTER SEVEN

GRISLY DISCOVERY

DECEMBER 31, 1984: NEAR THE TOWN OF
SUNDERLAND, ON, IN DURHAM REGION,
56 KM FROM QUEENSVILLE

Two months later, on a crisp New Year's Eve afternoon in
1984, Fred Patterson looked out of an upstairs bedroom
window. He saw the family's German Shepherd barking
and playing keep-away with another dog. They were in a
field a couple of kilometres away.

"Let's go for a walk," he called to his two daughters.
"We need to round up the dog before the snow storm
gets here."

Fred drove his vehicle around to the other end of
the field, and started walking in on the old tractor path
bordering it. He loved the peaceful and beautiful area.
Coming around the bend in the path, he saw a trailer
standing empty. The owner of the property lived in

Toronto and only used the trailer as a vacation spot a few times throughout the year. As they approached, Fred realized the trailer had been broken into. A window had been smashed and there were papers and things scattered on the ground. Some of the tall, overgrown grass was trampled. A few metres off the path, Fred saw a pile that looked like garbage. The dogs were running around the pile barking and pulling at something. Fred felt uneasy.

"Girls, stay on the path here while I get the dog," he said as he walked over to the dogs and the pile. His dog was forgotten when he reached the pile in the grass. He stood there for a moment and stared. His mind didn't want to accept what his eyes were seeing. At his feet laid the decomposed body of a child. She was on her back with her sweater pulled over her head, but the head wasn't attached to the body. Her neck had been severed. He felt like throwing up. The legs were spread apart strangely and some of the bones looked chewed on by animals. Other bits of the remains were scattered around the area. The child was only half dressed and next to the feet were a pair of Nike running shoes, blue corduroy pants, a belt, and a pair of girls' underpants.

Horrified, Fred grabbed his dog by the collar and took his kids home to call the Durham Regional Police.

"I really can't understand why I'd never seen it

before," Fred told the officers when they arrived at his home. "I must have drove, I figure, between four and five times past that body. And it must have been there at that particular time, but I never seen it. My neighbour drove up there, too, and he never seen anything."

It was 1:30 p.m. when the officers started arriving at the body site. Vehicle after vehicle arrived, along with vans, cars, trucks, and a hearse. The police parked their cruisers at an angle, where the tractor path met the road, to block off the entrance to the field. Soon the area was littered with activity. Inspector Robert Brown, in charge of the Durham Police Crimes Against Persons Squad, organized a ground search of the immediate area. The wind had a bite to it, and while the storm hadn't arrived yet, they all knew it was coming. They had to work fast if they were to process the area before it started snowing.

Sergeant Michael Michalowsky, Chief Identification Technician with the Durham Regional Police, arrived shortly after 2 p.m. in the identification van. He hung a bag on the side mirror, so searchers could dispose of coffee cups, food wrappers, and cigarette butts before entering the search area. Some of the officers ignored it or forgot to use it during the search.

It was Michalowsky's job to make sure everything was photographed where it was found, bagged, and tagged with the date and the case file.

"Of all the times to find a body, it had to be on the busiest night of the year," one of the officers mumbled to himself.

None of the officers were issued gloves, scarves, or protective clothing to prevent hair and fibres from falling on the remains and contaminating the evidence. Michalowsky was in a hurry, racing against the weather. It was going to be tough to get the search done before the storm.

The area around the body was quickly roped off with bright yellow police tape. It didn't take long before reporters and photographers arrived, shouting questions like:

"Who is it? Do you know yet?"

"Is she alive? Is it Christine?"

"Have you any information?"

The reporters yelled questions as the police went about their grisly work. Flash bulbs went off as photographers took pictures. The police ignored the group. They didn't have time to answer questions. The sky was darkening and, on the horizon, storm clouds were starting to gather. The site was exposed. If the police didn't work quickly, the storm could destroy evidence identifying the killer — if it was a murder scene. For all they knew at that moment, it could have been a lost child who had died of exposure. It would be too cruel to think of a child dying that way, only a kilometre or two from people's homes.

"I found something," an officer called. Michalowsky took his camera and snapped a picture of a cigarette butt in the long grass. "Over here," someone else yelled. Michalowsky quickly put the butt in a bag and stuffed it into his pocket. *I'll add this to the list in my notebook when I have a chance,* he thought to himself.

"What did you find?"

"Some buttons, maybe from the kid's blouse." Click went the camera, into the bag went the buttons. Then off to the next item.

The coroner arrived at about 4 p.m. The wind was blowing in small gusts. The bite in the air increased. They tried to work quickly, but time and weather were working against them. Twilight was quickly turning into darkness. The speed of the search increased. Only some of the items found were photographed properly and almost nothing was being written down.

The Brock Fire Department brought generators and floodlights so the searchers could see.

"Inspector Brown," said Fitzpatrick to his boss, "shouldn't we get a tarp or a tent to cover the area so we aren't so rushed? Then we can come back later when the storm has blown over."

"No," Brown replied. "We have enough time; we just have to work fast."

They took pictures of the body and the area around the body next. Normally a grid is laid out using twine and wooden pegs pounded into the ground, forming square sections. Each section is assigned to one person and when it is done being searched, it is crossed off the list. But there wasn't a grid, or twine, or pegs, or a list. No one had an assigned section to search.

"Quickly, people. Cover as much ground as you can. We haven't much time," Brown instructed them.

Some of the officers took smoke breaks and no one watched to make sure the cigarette butts were put in the trash bag hanging on the van mirror. A cigarette package, a sales receipt, and a milk carton were found close to the body. Those in charge decided these items didn't have anything to do with the murder, and they were thrown away. Other items were photographed, tagged, bagged, sent to the lab for analysis, and accepted as evidence, even though they were dropped by the searchers.

The body itself received special attention. All the clothing in the vicinity was carefully lifted, tagged, and placed in plastic bags, including the dirt and debris that may have been on the items. The officers then turned to the body itself. It took a half hour for the police to loosen it from the frozen ground, using shovels, before it was lifted onto a plywood board for transporting. The body started falling apart with the lifting. Bones fell onto the ground and were left there, forgotten. Those that were seen were picked up by bare hands and put back. No one seemed to notice. They were rushed for time.

The board, with its precious cargo, was put into a hearse and taken to the coroner's office in Toronto. And not too soon; the searchers had run out of time. The bad weather hit fast and hard. Before the mad scramble for the vehicles, Michalowsky picked up a cloth bag that lay next to the remains. A silence fell over the group as he carefully extracted a white recorder from the bag. As the first few flakes of snow fell from the sky, he read aloud the name taped to the side of the instrument. "Christine Jessop," he said.

8

CHAPTER EIGHT

THE MURDER INVESTIGATION BEGINS

DECEMBER 31, 1984

Robert Jessop, who had been granted an early release because of his daughter's disappearance, opened the door when the police came to their home. Janet, with dark circles under her eyes, trembled as her husband put his arm around her. They all went into the sitting room: the Jessops sitting nervously on the couch, the officers uncomfortably on chairs. Robert and Janet both broke down at the news that Christine's body had been found.

Christine had been their miracle child. They had adopted Kenny because doctors had told Janet she couldn't have any children. Then she had given birth to Christine. Now they knew for certain that their miracle, their little girl, would never walk through the door again.

News reporters interviewed the Jessops later that day. Janet sat awkwardly on Christine's bed next to her husband. With pink pillows and a little-girl bedspread as a backdrop, Janet looked at the floor and mindlessly twisted a tissue in her hands. Robert answered the reporter's questions in a monotone voice that sounded detached from his body. His arm around his wife lay there unmoving, forgotten.

"The devastation of the not-knowing, is really what tears you apart," Robert told reporters. "The unknown that we go through daily, the unknown part is really the most difficult for everyone in the family. It's a difficult . . . it's a difficult thing to accept. At least we know, we have her back."

• • •

That night, when the storm hit with driving wind, rain, snow, sleet, and ice, the police had no choice but to abandon the crime scene with the hope that the area had been searched enough. The storm raged throughout the night and all through the next day, leaving a blanket of snow fifteen to twenty centimetres deep. Underneath that clean and bright blanket of white lay evidence of a horror that had ended with the murder of a nine-year-old girl. Did the police find all the clues the murderer left behind, or was something missed? Something that could have told them who had committed this appalling crime?

During the storm, officers Michalowsky and Robinet returned to the Durham Regional Police station with the bagged items collected from the body site. Since the remains were found in the Durham Region, the case now belonged to them. The York police were asked to turn over everything they had.

The bagged items were hung up to dry. Brown Kraft wrapping paper was placed beneath the items to catch any fibres or hair or dirt particles that fell from them. Since most of the searchers hadn't worn gloves or protective clothing, any hair or fibres belonging to them were also caught by the paper. This mistake would have horrible consequences in the search for Christine's killer. The items were photographed, wrapped in the brown paper, tagged, placed in paper bags, and sent to the Ontario Centre of *Forensic* Sciences (CFS) in central Toronto for analysis.

The dental records confirmed what everyone already knew: the remains were Christine Jessop's.

The autopsy was performed by Dr. John Hillsdon-Smith, assisted by six others, including Sergeant Michalowsky and two other officers. Michalowsky removed the necklace from Christine's neck, and found some hairs, which he photographed and bagged. They all belonged to Christine except one. A single hair was later referred to as "the necklace hair." It was decided that this hair must have belonged to the killer.

The autopsy report showed that Christine had been beaten and stabbed. Some of the wounds were made to hurt and scare her, but not to kill her. Semen was found on the underpants, which had been lying next to the body. This suggested she had been attacked while dressed, and then again after they had been removed. There was a grey turtleneck at the body site that didn't belong to Christine. Did the turtleneck belong to another child in the killer's home?

"There is so much blood in the clothing, and yet almost none in the dirt from around the body," said the medical examiner. "Perhaps she hadn't been killed at the body site and even if she had been killed elsewhere, she couldn't have been dragged since that would have spread the blood further."

There were only a few answers, but so many more questions.

The medical examiner failed to take an inventory of the bones, or even clean the ones he had to check for more injuries. He noted in his findings that: "[The killer] slashed her throat with such force that she was nearly decapitated."

The doctor kept five bones in case more information

was needed after the body was buried. He eventually turned them over to the police. They were presumably filed with the rest of the case, but the bones disappeared, adding to the list of missing information.

The police canvassed the nearest neighbours to the body site, to see if anyone had noticed anything unusual on the day or evening of the little girl's disappearance. Lydia Robertson and some of her neighbours told of the late-night calls for help over twenty-four hours after Christine disappeared.

The police performed screaming tests to see if it would be possible for the neighbours to hear a child's scream from that distance. An officer stayed at the body site and talked and screamed a number of times, while other officers stood at the different houses and listened to see what could be heard. Even though the tests proved the sound could travel that far, the detectives decided it wasn't Christine the neighbours had heard. They simply didn't believe anyone could or would keep a nine-year-old against her will for longer than a few hours without someone finding out.

The neighbours' reports were ignored.

9

CHAPTER NINE

TUNNEL VISION

JANUARY 7, 1985

Christine's funeral service was held at the Queensville
United Church. Media vehicles lined the streets, camera
crews interviewed Queensville residents and police officers, and live reports were filmed in hushed tones. The
police were convinced the murderer would come to the
funeral, so they watched for anything suspicious. With all
the hype, it was difficult for the mourners to concentrate.
Many of them looked at their friends and neighbours,
and wondered if they could be the killer. Few heard the
words the minister spoke, or the stories shared, or the
scriptures read. They were too busy trying to figure out
which of them was the killer.

The body of Christine Jessop, along with her favourite Cabbage Patch doll, was buried in the Queensville
cemetery on January 7, 1985, in a plot about a hundred

metres behind her home. Many of those present knew Christine had loved to play in the cemetery. More than a few of them wondered if she, while playing her games, had walked on the plot of ground she was being buried under.

After the burial there was a small, private gathering in the Jessop home for family and a few close friends.

"So where are the Morins?" someone whispered. "Why weren't they at the funeral?"

"Mr. and Mrs. Morin are out of town on a cruise," someone else answered. "But Guy Paul is at home. Where was he today?"

"I heard he hadn't even helped with the search or even gave condolences to Janet and Robert."

Before Christine's body was found, the Morins, while respecting the Jessop family's privacy, had offered them support in many ways. On October 4, 1984, Alphonse Morin went with the Jessops to search for Christine. In November, before Christine's body was found, Guy Paul went to the Jessop home and sat with Robert Jessop for a half hour, just talking. After arriving home from their cruise and hearing about Christine's funeral, Ida and Alphonse called on the Jessops to offer their condolences.

"He has always been a bit strange . . . but you would have thought . . . the Jessops are his neighbours after all."

Guy Paul didn't know funerals were open to the public.

His absence was noted by the police. It seemed Guy Paul couldn't do anything right. The police and reporters believed the murderer would go to the funeral. If Guy Paul had gone, they would have noticed him, and perhaps thought he was guilty. But he didn't go, and they thought it was suspicious he stayed away.

While gathered in the living room at the Jessop home, at about 7 p.m., the guests were all startled to hear a man screaming for help. It sounded as though it was coming from the cemetery behind the house. Janet immediately ran outside. She later told police she saw the silhouette of a person walking quickly through the back door of the Morin house. She said she called out to the person, asking if she could help, but there was no answer. She also said she was certain it was Guy Paul Morin.

Detectives Fitzpatrick and Shephard met with Janet and Kenny Jessop on February 14, 1985. When asked about Guy Paul, they both said he was a musician and a "weird-type guy." They complained that he had never helped with the search for Christine and didn't attend the funeral or even give them his sympathies. Inspector John Shephard made an entry in his notebook identifying Guy Paul as "Suspect Morin."

Guy Paul Morin's name kept coming up. He was

beginning to stand out. The officers decided it was time to talk to the "weird-type guy" who lived next door. First, they wanted to do some digging. They started with Christine's best friend, Leslie Chipman.

"So Leslie," the detective asked, "tell me about Christine's neighbour, Guy Paul Morin. You said you were friends with Christine."

"Yeah, she was my best friend."

"So, when you were playing over there at Christine's and you saw Guy Paul, what was he doing?"

"I don't know," said Leslie.

"Well," said the detective, "was he cutting his lawn?"

"No."

"Was he standing next to his fence?"

"Yes."

"Could he have been cutting his hedges?"

"Yeah, I think so. He must have been cutting his hedges."

"Well," asked the detective, "was he holding the clippers tight?"

"Well," Leslie said. "I don't know."

"Well," pushed the detective, "were his knuckles white, did they look like this?" and he held out his fist so his knuckles looked white.

"Yeah, sure. Okay. Yes, it did look like that."

Fitzpatrick and Shephard made a note that Guy Paul's bedroom window looked down on the Jessops' backyard. Had he stood at that window and watched Christine playing? What was he thinking as he watched her? Is that when he decided to take her and kill her?

Fitzpatrick and Shephard wanted to speak to Guy Paul alone, without his parents in the way. So they had someone call him to get him out of the house.

"Hello, is this Guy Paul Morin?" a woman's voice inquired on the telephone.

"Yeah."

"I'm calling from the motor vehicle office in Toronto. There's a problem with your driver's licence and we need you to come in and sort it out. What time would be good for you?"

"There's no time good for me. It's your problem, not mine. I'm not going to waste my time helping you sort out your problem," said Guy Paul, and hung up the phone.

The officers couldn't believe it. Who refuses a request from the motor vehicle office? Did he suspect it was a setup?

So the officers parked down the street and watched for a couple of days, waiting for Ida and Al Morin to leave Guy Paul alone at the house. It didn't happen and they started getting frustrated, wondering if Guy Paul knew they were watching him. Finally, on February 22, 1985, they decided to take a chance. They wanted to see if they could at least get Guy Paul to come outside to talk to them in the police cruiser so the parents couldn't interfere. As the officers walked up to the Morins' back door, Guy Paul came outside to meet them.

"Hey, guys," he said to the officers. "Mom's asleep, this isn't a good time."

"Sure, we understand," they said, "but we don't need to talk to your mother. Can we have a few words with you? We could sit in the cruiser if you want, so we don't have to disturb her."

"Sure," Guy Paul answered.

Guy Paul jumped into the back seat and looked around. He had a big smile on his face, like a kid. Shephard slipped his hand into the briefcase on the front seat and turned on a tape recorder. There was a ninety-minute tape in it — more than enough time for the interview, he thought. Only he thought it would automatically reverse at the end of the first side. It didn't, and they lost forty-five minutes of the interview.

"Guy Paul," asked Fitzpatrick, "you smoke?" The officers knew there were cigarette butts found at the body site, and they were looking for a suspect who smoked.

Guy Paul was living next door to Christine so he would know her schedule. He was also a bit on the strange side, and seemed almost excited to be sitting in the police car. He chatted with them like they were all old friends.

"Nope."

"Do you mind if I do?" Guy Paul shook his head. Shephard made a notation in his notebook: *Doesn't smoke?*

After a friendly bit of chit-chat, Shephard asked Guy Paul if he preferred to be called Guy or simply Paul. Morin chuckled and said either one. Some called him Paul and some called him Guy. If they wanted, they could call him Guy Paul. It really didn't matter to him.

Shephard and Fitzpatrick wondered if Morin had two personalities: one called Guy and one called Paul. If so, which one was the killer?

"So, Guy Paul," said Shephard. "The night Christine went missing, you and your father were doing renovations, right? Can you tell me what you saw that night?"

"Sure. Okay, so it's starting to turn dark, so it's easily seven-thirty. I saw the first cop car. I said, 'Hey there's a cop car up there. Something must be going on, eh?' Dad said, 'Probably not, maybe another complaint.' You know we've got complaints, eh. When you do construction you get a little noisy, eh. Sometimes you get the odd bitching. The Jessops are super; I know that for a fact. Bob comes around and helps the odd time, eh. But, I said, 'Something must be going on.' The next one came up . . . and you know, for some reason and I . . . I'm really good when it comes to prediction, I said 'I bet that little Christine is gone.' Dad says, 'Christine, do you think? Nah, maybe Ken, something [else] maybe. You know, Ken's at the age, you know, just socializing. Maybe Ken's at that age when he's starting to get into trouble, eh?'"

"Um hum," said Fitzpatrick.

"But he's a super guy supposedly, eh. The parents say," said Guy Paul.

"Well," said Shephard.

"He has an ambition to be a doctor," continued Guy Paul. "Then another guess and another and another. And then it became a charade around here. And then we found out . . . Ken and the officer came and said 'Did you see Christine? And I said 'Holy shit, Dad . . .'" Guy Paul looked at the officers. "Why did I predict that? I . . . I didn't know she —"

"That's what I was going to ask you," said Fitzpatrick quietly, looking Guy Paul in the eyes.

"I don't know."

"What made that jump to your mind?"

"For some reason, I'm so close to many things," said Guy Paul. "I predict, eh —"

"So Guy Paul, do you work every day?" asked Shephard.

"Yeah, I love woodworking and Interiors International Limited is the best. The furniture ... beautiful veneer work like I've never seen. Amazing for woodworking, like it's real super-custom. There's a long table like twelve-feet long, easy. Joined together in the middle, certain beautiful anchor clips. They're far out in things today."

"Yeah," said Fitzpatrick. Then there was quiet. The officers looked at each other, and there was a long pause. He didn't smoke, so maybe the butts at the body site were there before the murder and didn't belong to the killer?

"Otherwise, I'm innocent." Guy Paul broke the silence. "But it's pretty bad how they treated [us,] the Regional. You know what they did around here. They said we're all guilty until proven otherwise."

"Who said that?" asked Fitzpatrick.

"Well it's not exactly what they said, but we're all suspects."

"Who's that, the Regional?"

"Yeah," answered Guy Paul.

"That's York?" said Fitzpatrick.

"That's York Regional, yeah. Isn't that bad, eh? How they portray us all as being guilty ... And they say: 'Hey we're going to be doing a door-to-door search' and you know what? They *only* did us."

"What?" said Shephard. "They searched your house?"

"No, a door-to-door," said Guy Paul. "Coming to the people and questioning and questioning and questioning. All right, so they been to see us more than once. You guys have already been here three times, eh?"

"Who was here? We've never been here," said Fitzpatrick.

"Joe, big boy."

"Oh, Loughlin."

"Well there was two of them like you, eh, but um, they were a little more brashish, eh. So they asked me for my phone number. I said, 'I don't give out my phone number, it's private, eh.' And he said, 'What in the hell are you saying, you don't give out your phone number?' And I said, 'Not even to the band members. There's only one who has it, some lady for the band if there's a cancellation due to weather or something.' And um, he said, 'For chrissakes, there's a missing child here!' And I said, 'What the hell does that have to do with my number?' and then he said, 'What the hell, you on drugs or what?' I said, 'Hey I never touch that shit.' I mean that's picky.

"Christine, ya know. She's a sweetheart. Two weeks before her disappearance, she came over to see my sister's puppy. She was more alive than Kenny. Sweet girl. I was wearing a veil and bees attacking me while I was sowing clover. Christine said to me, 'Are you sowing honey seeds?' Very, very innocent kid. She never heard me play the saxophone.

"The news was wrong, eh?" Guy Paul continued. "They said she was found west of Queensville, but she was found across the Ravenshoe Road."

Fitzpatrick and Shephard exchanged a glance. How did he know the fastest way to get to the body site from Queensville was along the Ravenshoe? It was a rough road, not a highly travelled route.

"I know that way, eh? My parents have a chunk of land on the Ravenshoe. That's where I moved my bees to, because of the complaints," said Guy Paul. The officers later found out that the Morins' property was over forty-five kilometres from the body site.

Next, the officers followed up with Morin's place of employment.

"No, he was late on the morning of October 3, 1984," Guy Paul's boss told the police. "That was unusual for him, being late. He also gave his notice in November, which was a surprise. I was sorry to lose him; he was an excellent worker but private-like. He didn't talk much to anyone and seemed to keep a distance from the other employees."

Morin's time card showed he left work at 3:32 p.m. on October 3, 1984. He lived 57.1 kilometres from work so it would have taken him forty-two minutes to get home, as long as he didn't make any stops. This meant he would have arrived home at 4:14 p.m. at the earliest.

Shephard and Fitzpatrick then went to the office of Kenny Jessop's dentist and asked when the Jessops had left their office.

"I'm pretty sure it was at least four-thirty before Janet finally came to pick him up. Kenny waited a long time in the reception area," said the dentist.

"I don't think it was that late," the receptionist said. "It was closer to four, more like four-ten or four-twenty."

Either way, the Jessops couldn't have arrived home until 4:34 p.m. at the earliest. This gave Morin enough time to snatch Christine.

Next, the investigators drove to Morin's house and, taking Ravenshoe Road, they timed the trip out to the body site. It took about thirty minutes. This meant it was possible for Guy Paul to leave work at 3:32, arrive home at 4:14, kidnap Christine, drive out to the body site, assault and kill her, and still make it home by 5:30 or 6 p.m. So Guy Paul must be lying about his shopping stops on his way home. Janet and Kenny Jessop couldn't have arrived home at 4:10 p.m. as they said. There had to be a reason why Janet was so adamant that they arrived home shortly after four. Guy Paul was most likely the one who had done this. He had the time and the opportunity. They were on the right trail, they just knew it.

"Janet," Fitzpatrick said later that day. "The dentist's office said you didn't leave there until closer to four-thirty the day Christine went missing. Are you certain of the time? Could your clock be slow?"

"I had a new watch," piped up Kenny, "it said four-ten. I looked at it."

"Janet?" prompted Shephard, ignoring Kenny. "Do you feel guilty for not being here when Christine got home from school? Could your clock have been slow?"

"Well," said Janet Jessop. "I suppose it was possible the clock could have been slow; we are having problems with the electric clock."

Fitzpatrick and Shephard looked at each other. They had the killer; it was Guy Paul Morin. Now, all they had to do was prove it.

CHAPTER TEN

THE PROFILE

APRIL 17, 1985

"*Profiling* is a great tool in giving direction to the police," said FBI profiler John Douglas. He was asked by the Durham police to prepare a profile of the killer of Christine Jessop.

"It's important that I receive untainted, objective information in order for the profile to be accurate. I need all the evidence and it's absolutely necessary that the police have no suspects in mind when compiling the information I need. Only then can the profile be a useful tool in identifying and obtaining a confession from the guilty party."

The Durham police assured the profiler that they had no suspects in mind, but failed to say they were already building a case against Guy Paul Morin. So the facts of the case forwarded to John Douglas were incomplete.

Criminal profiling takes the details and clues of a crime and compares them with similar crimes that have been solved. The similarities and the differences help point to the type of person that may have committed the crime. It isn't meant to pinpoint an individual, but to give the police a direction to look in.

The following are only a few of the characteristics Mr. Douglas identified in his profile:

- The victim sought out someone she knew and trusted to show him the recorder she had received that day;
- The offender was youthful, late teens, early twenties;
- He was having personal problems at home, school, or work and was experiencing many life stresses, and may have had difficulties with a girlfriend at the time of the offence;
- Not antisocial, but somewhat of a loner who prefers his own company;
- May present a façade as a macho individual, superior to others, but has poor self-esteem and lacks self-confidence;
- Tends to play with children who might be impressed by his antics;

- Drives older-model vehicle, not well-maintained, and cruises area in vehicle, spends time cruising in his car as a vehicle for escape;
- Has a poor self-image and may have a physical ailment, disability, or disfigurement or facial scars and does not maintain good personal hygiene, is not well-groomed, needs a haircut or shave, wears sloppy, soiled clothing in need of repair;
- Will have a criminal history of nuisance, arson, cruelty to animals, voyeurism, or break and entering;
- Lazy, not a high-achiever, of average intelligence, a mediocre student; offenders of this type generally do not graduate from high school, but if he did, he would have gotten by with barely passing grades;
- May have cleaned the car's interior after the offence;
- Rigid, stiff, pre-occupied, or nervous with the police;
- Overly co-operative, participated in searches, which show how concerned he is;
- Has difficulty sleeping.

Although parts of the profile fitted Guy Paul Morin, parts didn't. For example, other than the neighbours' noise complaints, he had never been in trouble with the law. He was not lazy; he didn't have a poor self-image or signs of an inflated ego. He didn't have a physical disability or obvious scars. He didn't cruise the neighbourhood in his car and his car hadn't been cleaned in months, perhaps even years. Guy Paul Morin was a very intelligent man and wasn't nervous or suspicious when speaking to the police. He may not have taken part in the official search for the missing girl, but he didn't have any difficulties at work, with his current girlfriend, or with his family. He dated girls close to his own age, not young girls, and didn't seem to have a history of being around children for company.

Nevertheless, the police investigators strongly believed that Guy Paul was the killer. They needed to make him nervous, get him to admit to it. So they took the FBI profile and made small changes in it to fit Guy Paul Morin. They had the new version of the profile published in the newspapers.

In the *Toronto Sun* on April 17, 1985: "Police released some details of an FBI report that gives a psychological portrait of Jessop's killer. According to the findings of FBI agent John Douglas, the killer is white, between nineteen and twenty-six years old, has a high school education and is intelligent, he's a night person, dresses sloppily, and feels superior to others. The FBI believes the man is a labourer, lives in Queensville, and knew and had the trust of Christine. It's believed he was sane and did not intend to commit murder, but lost control after sexually assaulting the girl. Police say they have less than five suspects in the case and are watching all closely."

"Guy Paul," said Al Morin from behind his copy of the *Toronto Sun*. "Come here, read this."

"The profile, Dad." said Guy Paul. "It sounds like me. They're crazy, Dad, you know I couldn't have possibly done this."

"It's like what they said on the news last week, Christ. You're the 'grubby sucker' around here. You've always been grubby," said Al Morin, teasing Guy Paul.

"Yeah, well, that's my way. And age, what, nineteen to twenty-six? That sounds like me," said Guy Paul. "There's no reason to think about it, Dad. I swear, this is so crazy."

11

CHAPTER ELEVEN

THE ARREST

APRIL 22, 1985

"Fitzpatrick, Shephard! Call's in," said dispatch at the Durham police station "Morin's a match, bring him in."

The police waited at the Queensville intersection for Guy Paul Morin on April 22, 1985. When Morin drove past them on his way to band practice, the cruiser flashed its lights and Morin pulled over. He thought it was a routine traffic stop, so he got out of the car and approached the police officers. He was surprised to see not the York police, but Detectives Fitzpatrick and Shephard from the Durham police. While he tried to remain friendly and casual, he was on edge from all the pressure and reactions from Queensville residents and even friends since the release of the profile in the papers. He knew he didn't do it, but he couldn't stop what other people thought.

"What's up, guys?" he asked. He could feel the sweat

on the palms of his hands.

"Mr. Guy Paul Morin, you are under arrest for the *first-degree murder* of Christine Jessop," John Shephard answered him.

Guy Paul's knees went weak and his stomach turned over. He was not prepared for this. "What!" he exclaimed. "You're kidding, John. Look, I'll be happy to answer your questions, just let me go to band practice first."

"Get in the car, Mr. Morin."

"You're trying to tell me I killed a child, a person. Get real!"

He was told his rights and six months after the abduction and murder of Christine Jessop, Guy Paul Morin was transported to the police department in Whitby for processing. The family Honda was impounded and towed to CFS. He was twenty-five years old.

The arrest was only one part of the officers' plan. Earlier that day they had obtained a search warrant for the Morin residence. As soon as the arrest was reported on the police band radio, police cars surrounded the house. Lights flashed; police officers poured into the yard and stood ready at each exit. The Morins were given the search warrant and the ransacking began. Tapes were used on the carpets to collect fibres, closets emptied, drawers turned upside down. Eighty-one items were seized from the home, including one dark grey fibre. The car was vacuumed and fibres were taken from the vacuum bags. (There is no record stating whether or not the vacuum bags were new or sterile before they were used in the Morin case. Therefore, there is no way of verifying which fibres in the bag were from the Morins' car.)

The police searched all night, yet they didn't find anything that was on their list: a yellow seat cover which could match yellow fibres they found on the body; buttons from Christine's blouse; red animal hairs; Christine's blue sweater; or the murder weapon.

On the way to the police station, Inspector Shephard turned on the tape recorder to record the conversation. The recorder malfunctioned and so the following is from notes made of the conversation.

"You really surprise me. You really do. You've made a mistake. You really have. I don't want you to make any mistakes, but you have. I never touched Christine, never," said Guy Paul.

"Guy, are you certain that you never touched her? That's a pretty broad statement," said Shephard.

"I know, John. Never. I never touched her. I mean that, I really do. Never, I never touched her."

"Never gave her a hug or a piggy-back ride, just playing with her?"

"Never. I never hugged her, never gave her a piggy-back ride. I never placed a hand on that girl."

"Guy," said Shephard, "I don't mean in a sexual way, I mean just playing with her or just in fun, maybe you picked her up and swung her around."

"John, I never touched her, never placed a hand on her," said Guy Paul.

"We got your hair on Christine, her hair in your car, plus fibres in your car and on her clothing. We also have fingerprints, Guy, and fingerprints don't lie."

"Fingerprints on what?" said Guy Paul.

"Guy, the Ontario Provincial Police tech support services in Toronto have the latest laser equipment for detecting fingerprints on clothing, skin, leather, and fingerprints don't lie," said Shephard, even though there were no fingerprints connecting Guy Paul to the murder of Christine Jessop.

Once they were at the 18 Division police station, Guy Paul handed over his penknife, which became evidence against him. Morin volunteered samples of his hair, blood, and saliva.

He refused to take a polygraph test.

"Listen, Guy Paul," the officer at the interview stated. "You could save your parents money in legal fees if you confess."

"I didn't do it."

Guy Paul sat in a chair in the interview room. It was a dream, a nightmare. His mind was not processing everything very well. There were filing cabinets in the room all bearing Christine's name, a map of Queensville with coloured lines on it, and a photograph of the murdered little girl. Next to the photo was a piece of paper indicating that a fingerprint connected with the crime scene had been positively identified as his. He was stunned. How was that possible?

Guy Paul didn't know this room had been staged as suggested by John Douglas, the FBI profiler who had given them the following instructions:

> *The interview should be conducted in a dimly lit room that looks like the headquarters of a task force. As he looks around the room he sees investigative flow charts and filing cabinets. His name is on one file cabinet and the victim's name is on another. He sees the underwear, clothing, and the recorder that belonged to the victim wrapped in clear plastic. There should be evidence envelopes labelled with positive ID, and labelled fingerprints laying in the open. These items should be placed off in a corner of a*

room where the subject will see them during the interview. Place the items in front of him when it appears he is becoming agitated and nervous.

The subject will be more willing to provide a confession at this point and you can expect him to break down and show remorse, even cry. This will not be genuine. His tears are not tears for the victim, but tears for himself because his life is now ruined. Deep down he has no remorse for this victim. His only remorse is that he is going to have to go to jail. [Not verbatim; edited for clarity.]

It was a long night. The same questions were asked repeatedly in different ways. The photo of Christine seemed to stare at him from across the room, her smile and eyes watching him.

"I didn't do it, guys," he kept saying, but they weren't listening. It was so frustrating not being able to make them understand. He knew he didn't do it. "I did *not* kill that little girl," he repeated over and over again.

"Do you smoke, Guy Paul?" asked the officer as he held out a cigarette to Guy Paul.

"No," said Guy Paul. "I've never smoked." The

officers looked at each other. This could be a problem. A cigarette package, lighter, and some butts were found at the body site. If Guy Paul didn't smoke then these items couldn't have anything to do with the murder.

"When did you arrive home from work on October third?"

"Between five-thirty and six o'clock."

"Which is it? Five-thirty or six o'clock?"

"I went shopping after work, I really didn't look closely at the time but the Jessops' car was in the driveway and my sister was there. It was around five-thirty, six o'clock."

The Jessops originally placed their arrival time that day at 4:10 p.m.

"It wasn't until I woke up the next morning with the imprint of a steel jail bed in my face that the enormity of my situation sank in. I was sort of hopeless at that point," said Morin at the Public Inquiry, years later. "I didn't have any control of anything except to proclaim my innocence and that's what I did all night. During the interrogation, I did my best to try and tell them that they got the wrong person. They didn't want to believe that. I fought for my innocence that night as I have over the years; I was fighting for my life."

While Guy Paul was being questioned at the station,

the search at the Morin house was underway. The paper bag of receipts Guy Paul kept in his room was dumped onto the floor and searched. If there had been grocery or gas receipts dated for October 3, they weren't in the bag when the police left and there were no reports of any found.

"Guy Paul *Moron*," laughed Shephard with another officer. "We've got him on this one."

12

CHAPTER TWELVE

PREPARING A DEFENCE

DECEMBER 1985

Al and Ida put up the money for Guy Paul's lawyers, Bruce Affleck and Alexander Sosna. Affleck and Sosna wanted to pursue an insanity plea. Guy Paul refused, stating over and over that he was innocent and he would not plead otherwise, but the lawyers were stubborn. Guy Paul finally lost patience and dismissed them in December 1985. Clayton Ruby was hired instead.

Clayton Ruby was an excellent and thorough defence attorney with a great team. He saw right away that this nerdy musician with his slightly quirky ways could be an easy target for police. If his neighbours and the police could jump to the conclusion that Guy Paul was the killer, how would the *jury* react to him? Ruby believed the Crown would portray Guy Paul as odd, perhaps even crazy. He decided they needed to face this head-on.

He insisted that Guy Paul see two psychiatrists as a condition of his representation. Guy Paul was furious and proclaimed his innocence yet again. Ruby assured him he believed in his innocence and was concerned what would happen to Guy Paul in prison if the jury found him guilty. A mental institution was better than prison if convicted of a child's sexual assault and murder. Guy Paul reluctantly agreed.

Psychologist Dr. Graham Turrall spent approximately fourteen hours with Guy Paul, administering numerous tests. Psychiatrist Dr. Basil Orchard examined Mr. Morin for approximately five to six hours. Both professionals diagnosed Guy Paul as having *simple schizophrenia*.

Ruby decided to use Guy Paul's medical diagnosis as his defence.

Guy Paul was horrified. He strongly opposed the suggestion that he would ever, could ever, kill a child. He wanted to plead not guilty, because he wasn't guilty. He was innocent.

Ruby was adamant. He knew that Guy Paul was innocent, but he knew jurors were only people. Faced with a next-door neighbour who everyone said was odd, and the Crown's long list of witnesses, Ruby knew they couldn't dismiss the possibility of a guilty *verdict*. Guy Paul argued relentlessly until they struck a compromise. They would plead not guilty and Ruby would lobby the court to allow him to use the insanity plea if, and only if, the jury finds Guy Paul guilty. The court denied his request. If the insanity plea was to be used at all, it had to be introduced in trial. Guy Paul didn't like it, but finally he agreed.

In preparation for trial, Clayton and his team went through the pictures of the body site. They asked to examine the cigarette butts found at the scene. Sergeant Michalowsky couldn't find the cigarette butts. They had disappeared. Sergeant Michalowsky decided to hide his original notes of the search and create a second note-book of the items found at the body site. The second notebook eliminated evidence that didn't match with Guy Paul's guilt. One cigarette butt that was originally recorded was turned into a curl of bark found in the long grass in the second notebook. The other cigarette butt was now recorded as belonging to one of the search-ers and had disappeared. The cigarette package in the original notebook was turned into a milk carton in the second notebook and had been recorded as thrown away. The date on the receipt found at the crime scene was too recent to be relevant to the murder, so this too was discarded.

Two convicted criminals approached the police. They said they had heard Guy Paul confess to the murder when he was in jail. They agreed that they would testify about the confession. In return they wanted to be released from jail and receive help with their court cases.

"We're ready for trial," decided the Crown.

Their mindset: The police have done their job and found the killer. Now we have to put him away for a long, long time.

CHAPTER THIRTEEN

THE FIRST TRIAL OF GUY PAUL MORIN

JANUARY 7, 1986: LONDON, ON, COURTHOUSE

The heavy wooden doors swung open to the waiting public. The courtroom smelled heavy with stale air mixed with wood polish. A hush fell on the waiting crowd of reporters, family members, and the curious as they took their seats. The defence counsel, Clayton Ruby and Mary Bartley, were wearing their barrister robes and were seated in the front of the courtroom on the left, behind long tables.

The *Crown attorneys,* John Scott and his assistant Susan MacLean, also in robes, sat on the right. Both groups faced the judge's box, the court reporter, and the court clerks. Amidst the sound of shuffling paper and the snap of briefcases, the accused, Guy Paul Morin, was led to the prisoner's box along the left wall. He sat and looked down at the floor, seemingly unaware of those around him. He looked nervous, pale, subdued, and had dark circles around his eyes.

Everyone stood as Justice McLeod Archibald Craig entered and was seated. The case was called, *motions* were heard, and then the jury filed in. They took their places in the jury box along the right wall, facing Guy Paul.

Defence lawyer Clayton Ruby entered a plea for his client:

"Not guilty, Your Honour."

The hush over the spectators seemed unnatural. Not only was this a fight for a young man's life, this was also about the murder of an innocent little girl. Emotions were high.

Christine's mother was sworn in as a witness.

John Scott (Crown attorney): On October 3, 1984, did you provide any information to the police relating to the time that you had thought you got home from the dentist?

Janet Jessop: Yes, I did.

Scott: And what time was that?

Jessop: Well, I know for a fact that at ten to five, I had to make a call to a lawyer in the city, which I did, and before that, as I say, we had looked around thoroughly and I had made a few phone calls, and I thought, which I could be wrong, it was around ten after, quarter after four I got home, but I could be wrong.

Scott: What information did you provide to the police that evening, if you recall, as to the time you got home?

Jessop: I think I told them around ten after, quarter after four.

Clayton Ruby approached the witness to conduct the cross-examination.

Clayton Ruby (defence): You said there was some uncertainty in your mind as to when you arrived home on the day of the disappearance. What is your best feeling about when you arrived home, leaving aside what others have said? Just what is your best recollection?

Janet Jessop: Well, not having a watch on that day, I'm going by the time I called the lawyer, and that was ten to five, and knowing what I did before I called, it wouldn't take me any more than maybe ten, fifteen minutes at the outside to look around the house, go outside, make a few phone calls to girlfriends. I couldn't have been at home much more than fifteen minutes, so maybe my timing is way out as far as what time I came home.

Ruby: Why are you sure about ten to five?

Jessop: Because I looked at the clock deliberately thinking I had to call this person at that time.

Ruby: And you think it was about fifteen minutes associated with looking around before you called?

Jessop: It couldn't have been more than that. Ten minutes at the most to look around the home. I went out the back and called, made a cup of coffee, and sat down.

Ruby: So tell me if I'm being correct and fair. You think it was ten to fifteen minutes you were there before making the phone call, making the coffee, looking around?

Jessop: Yes.

Ruby: Ten to fifteen minutes?

Jessop: Yes.

It was the Crown's theory that Guy Paul left work on October 3, 1984, arrived home about 4:30 p.m., lured Christine Jessop into his car, and took her to the body site in Durham Region where he sexually assaulted and killed her before returning home to Queensville.

Ruby: Time card showed Guy Paul left work at 3:32 p.m., did some shopping, bought a lottery ticket, and filled up with gas and arrived home between 5:30 and 6:00, verified by his parents.

The defence argued that Guy Paul's movements on October 3, 1984, made it impossible for him to have committed the murder.

Shortly after the trial began, a contamination was discovered at the Hair and Fibre Analysis department at CFS. The scientist working on the Jessop case had discovered that the hair-and-fibre samples taken from the Morins' house and car, as well as the samples from the body and the victim's clothing, had been contaminated in the lab or possibly by a searcher at the body site. The head of the department was notified, but the information was not passed on to either the defence or the prosecution. The trial continued and the *expert testimony* was given by CFS employees Ms. Nyznyk and Mr. Erickson.

The court was told that, "Ms. Nyznyk [the forensic analyst] had concluded that the necklace hair and samples of Mr. Morin's head hairs were consistent with coming from the same source."

The trial ended on February 7, 1986. During the closing arguments, Defence counsel Clayton Ruby and Crown Attorney John Scott both stated that Guy Paul Morin was mentally ill. Ruby added that the jury, made up of seven men and five women, should only consider his mental condition if they believed he was guilty of the murder.

"My client is simply a quiet Queensville musician who happens to be quietly schizophrenic. You can safely act on that evidence," he said, "but only if you are first satisfied beyond any reasonable doubt that he did it, that he committed this offence . . . Have they got the right man?" Ruby asked, "Or have they merely got the crazy neighbour? That's the problem."

The Crown's speech to the jury included:

"It may well be a situation where you find that Guy Paul Morin is the person who killed that little girl. He is, but the crime is so horrendous, so beyond what we can imagine a person could commit, that he must be an insane person."

Before the jury was excused from the courtroom to make their decision on the case, the judge spoke to them as well.

After thirteen hours of deliberation, the jury found Morin not guilty. He was free after fifty weeks in custody on the first-degree murder charge.

Guy Paul was elated. He started to put his life back together and figure out what he was going to do for work. He had met a file clerk named Fiona, and they started dating. He could finally breathe again.

14

CHAPTER FOURTEEN

PREPARING FOR A NEW TRIAL

JUNE 1987-MARCH 1990

His freedom was brief. The Crown appealed the *verdict* on the basis that the jury had been wrongly instructed by the judge, which could have influenced their decision. The Crown won their appeal. In the United States someone cannot be tried twice for the same crime (called Double Jeopardy). There is no such law in Canada, so Guy Paul Morin was ordered to stand trial, for the second time, for the murder of Christine Jessop.

On June 7, 1987, he was once again in custody. A friend said Morin was in tears when told of the ruling.

"This really is a nightmare," the friend quoted him as saying. "When will it end?"

Legal papers and motions flew back and forth. Both camps reorganized and rebuilt their arguments. Witnesses were notified and re-interviewed and evidence re-examined.

The trial preparations dragged on for years. Crown accused the defence of dragging their feet. They were right. The defence was scrambling to reassemble the arguments, evidence, and witnesses.

In March 1990, the new identification officer met with Crown Attorney Susan MacLean to go over the evidence of the Jessop case. He had the case file and a box of material left behind by Sergeant Michalowsky when he left on sick leave. While going through the boxes, they found the two notebooks. At first they thought it was simply a duplicate in case the original notebook was misplaced. They sat down and started to compare the entries. They were different. It appeared the second notebook was made either to cover up mistakes, or to get rid of evidence that didn't fit with their case against Guy Paul.

The cigarette butts collected at the body site had been thrown out, as had a lighter, a cigarette package, and a credit card receipt that were also bagged at the crime scene. Before the second trial, the defence asked to examine the cigarette butts found at the scene. Trying to cover up the fact that he had destroyed the original cigarette butts, Michalowsky gave them a cigarette butt to look at, saying he thought it was lost but he had actually found it under the flap of a box. Defence asked examiners to compare the cigarette butt to the brand that the officer smoked. It was different. No tests were done on the original cigarette butts before they had been thrown out, so no one would ever know if they had come from the real killer. Guy Paul didn't smoke.

Michalowsky was caught in the lie, and before the second trial he was charged with perjury (lying on the stand at trial) and two counts of wilfully attempting to obstruct, pervert, or defeat the course of justice.

What Guy Paul Morin and his family went through during this time was horrible. Guy Paul was innocent, but the authorities wouldn't listen. He and his family were treated like criminals by friends and neighbours. Guy Paul was living among neighbours who believed he not only murdered a nine-year-old girl, but that he had also done terrible things to her.

The Jessops were also victims. They lost their little Chrissy and the grief was at times almost overwhelming. Kenny Jessop had nightmares and many sleepless nights. He kept begging his parents to take him to the place his sister was found. It was hard for his parents, but finally they agreed, hoping this would help Kenny sleep at night.

It was unsettling to walk to the place where Christine had been found. The trees had grown and the grass was taller. Birds sang in the trees, and it looked so peaceful. They approached the place where she had lain. Flowers someone had put on the spot were dried and brown. Kenny knelt down and felt the hollow in the earth where the police had taken the body and the dirt away. He felt something hard, and pulled out a long bone. He looked at his mother, who started to cry. Robert ran to the car and came back with a Styrofoam cup to put the bone in. Then Kenny found another, and then another.

They didn't know for sure if the bones belonged to Christine, but they all believed they did. Solemnly, Kenny sat in the back seat of the car, holding the bones all the way to the police station. CFS confirmed they did indeed belong to Christine. During the autopsy, the doctor had failed to make an inventory of the remains. No one could be sure that even with these bones, they had found them all. If the doctor had missed this, then what else had he missed?

The body of Christine Jessop was exhumed in order to conduct a second autopsy and take an inventory of the bones. The Jessop family stood by as the coffin containing the little girl was uncovered.

"I'm very upset. I just wanted them to leave her alone," said Kenny Jessop.

The second autopsy was done by two new doctors and showed the initial autopsy was incomplete. The bones found by the Jessops were in fact Christine's and there were still some missing. New findings included wounds made in an attempt to cut the body up into pieces. They also found indications that the victim put up a struggle and it would have taken the killer at least thirty minutes to inflict the injuries. This information changed the timeline. Neither of the doctors could see how these findings had been missed in the original autopsy. What other mistakes had been made?

15

CHAPTER FIFTEEN

ON TRIAL AGAIN

NOVEMBER 13, 1991

The second trial began. Leo McGuigan was the head *prosecutor* with Susan MacLean assisting. Mr. McGuigan was tough and tenacious.

In his opening remarks, Jack Pinkofsky, Guy Paul's new defence lawyer, a beefy man with a cascade of white curls, told the jury the Crown's case was built on a "quicksand of speculation," bungled police work, and "no real evidence."

The retrial lasted nearly nine months and 120 witnesses were called.

Morin's alibi was the strong point of his defence and the insanity defence was thrown out. His father and his mother were his witnesses confirming that he arrived home at 5:30 or 6 p.m. But the defence were blindsided when Kenny and Janet Jessop changed their stories. Both testified they arrived home at 4:30 or even later, saying the mix-up was because their kitchen clock was wrong and they had thrown it out shortly after Christine went missing. (A re-enactment of Christine's disappearance that appeared on television before Guy Paul's original arrest clearly showed the clock still on the kitchen wall, showing the time as 4:10 as they walked into the house.) The new *testimony* appeared to show that Guy Paul had plenty of time to leave work at 3:32 p.m., pick up Christine, assault her and kill her, and still get home by 5:30 or 6 p.m.

The receipts showing Guy Paul had been grocery shopping had disappeared.

As in the first trial, the lottery salesperson could not be sure Guy Paul had bought a lottery ticket that Wednesday, stating that he came most Wednesdays, but not every Wednesday. Even with fabricated and missing evidence, without his alibi, it was a slam dunk for the Crown. Any other evidence was gravy, produced to seal the deal.

The Crown decided not to call Sergeant Michalowsky, since he was under investigation for his mishandling of evidence. However, the defence decided to call him to testify *because* he was under investigation.

Michalowsky's personal counsel objected and

produced medical letters from his doctors advising that the trial could put too much stress on his heart condition. Justice Donnelly ordered him to testify and made allowances to relieve as much of the stress as possible. No one was permitted to wear robes, his doctor would stay by his side and monitor his condition, and everyone would stay seated. Michalowsky sat behind a screen with his back to the spectators. The judge went even further; he shook Michalowsky's hand and welcomed him to the courtroom.

"It's nice to see you again," the judge said to him.

Defence was outraged. They stated the judge's concessions and actions made the jury sympathize with Michalowsky.

"I'm not sure of all of it. I'm not sure of anything. I'm really not sure why I'm even here," said Michalowsky to the court.

Due to the judge's attitude, the defence couldn't examine the witness properly. Calling Michalowsky under these circumstances did more harm to Guy Paul Morin than good.

The prosecution called the two jailhouse informants who had testified at the first trial. Robert Dean May, a fellow inmate of Morin's in Whitby Jail, testified that Guy Paul Morin had confessed to him that he had murdered Christine Jessop. As well, there was a statement from a

Mr. X, whose identity was protected, who witnessed the confession from the cell beside Guy Paul's.

May testified at both trials. He swore he heard Guy Paul Morin say, "I killed her, I killed that little girl."

May had a substantial criminal record and admitted that he had a problem. He desperately wanted to be released from jail and would do whatever was necessary to accomplish this. He told the police he would implicate other inmates. At the second trial, May was diagnosed by mental health experts as being a pathological liar with a deficient social conscience.

Mr. X was in jail for sexual assault and had a lengthy criminal record. His crimes were often against young children and yet when asked why he testified, he said he was outraged at what Morin had done to the victim. In 1988, he was diagnosed with a personality disorder which included sociopathic tendencies. An expert at the trial testified that this is characterized by exaggeration, lying, suggestibility, and disregard for social norms.

Mr. X stated on the witness stand, "and I overheard some discussions in the cell next to me. And I heard someone weeping, and I kind of paid a little more attention. And the voice got a little louder, and I heard 'I killed her, I killed that little girl.' And it's my belief that it came from Mr. Morin."

The court was told that both May and X passed polygraph tests (lie-detector tests). Then the polygraphist warned the court not to place too much confidence in the test.

As in the first trial, hair-and-fibre evidence was introduced to the court. Not only was the contamination withheld at this trial as well, the CFS representatives, Ms. Nyznyk and Mr. Erickson, again testified without mentioning it. This contamination made all of the fibre-and-hair findings useless. Yet, it was the false report on the fibre-and-hair evidence that had elevated Guy Paul Morin to prime suspect in this case.

Guy Paul took the stand in his own defence.

"Did you have anything to do with the disappearance and death of Christine Jessop?" Morin's lawyer asked.

"Not a thing at all," Morin replied. He then described the frustration of being accused of something he didn't do, and the stress that was put on his family. His bitterness washed over him, and at times his voice shook with emotion.

"I never expected I would have to go to trial. I can't believe it's still going on." He appeared to choke back tears when he explained a visit from his father and brother while in jail and realized, "I was missing all the things I'd be able to do myself. That was probably the saddest time. Here I am in jail for something I had nothing to do with."

In the closing arguments, the Crown reminded the jury that the jailhouse informants refused a deal for their testimony, saying it showed the court that the witnesses weren't bribed or forced and therefore were unmotivated to lie. Years later, the Inquiry found evidence of favours the Crown did for the two informants for years after they testified against Guy Paul. In truth, Guy Paul didn't confess in the jail cell, or anywhere else. The two informants lied about an innocent man so they could get out of jail for the crimes they were guilty of.

In his closing arguments, Leo McGuigan also stated (regarding the hair-and-fibre evidence): "both Mr. Erickson and Ms. Nyznyk formed an expert scientific opinion that all three hairs located in the accused's car were similar to the known hairs of Christine Jessop and could have originated from that source. As I said to you earlier, ladies and gentlemen of the jury, dealing with the examination of hair, it doesn't get any better than that."

After sitting through a nine-month trial, the jury deliberated for only seven days. Court was called for July 30, 1992, to hear the verdict.

Guy Paul sat in the prisoner's box, motionless and expressionless, as the foreman read the verdict: "Guilty of first-degree rape and murder of Christine Jessop."

Alphonse Morin's face went white at the words condemning his innocent son, and Guy Paul's girlfriend, Fiona, burst into tears. At the defence table, Jack Pinkofsky put his head in his hands as the rest of the team wiped away tears.

Guy Paul Morin was sentenced to twenty-five years.

"I'm not guilty of this crime," a tired-looking Morin, now thirty-two years old, told Justice James Donnelly in a firm voice as he leaned forward to stand in the prisoner's box.

"It's a travesty of justice," Morin said later to reporters, flanked by his lawyer. "I'm appealing this, that's all I have to say."

"He is innocent and has been from day one," said Guy Paul's sister, Denise.

The Jessops were relieved. They smiled, hugged, and cried. *At last*, they thought.

"Finally, the guilty one has paid for Christine's murder," Janet Jessop said. "I was convinced. I knew he had done it and it was just a matter of time until justice took its course."

"It's been a long eight years," Bob Jessop said. "The only consolation of the whole affair is that it's finally put to rest."

"I know I'm not the killer. They can say all they want," Morin told CBC's *the fifth estate.*

After the trial, a jury member told reporters she thought Guy Paul was guilty because he didn't look any of the jury in the eyes during the trial.

The prosecutor, Leo McGuigan, went to his favourite bar after Guy Paul was convicted and celebrated his win with his favourite beer.

He celebrated too soon.

16

WAITING FOR JUSTICE

AUGUST 1992-FEBRUARY 1993

Guy Paul Morin was taken to the Kingston Penitentiary. He was stripped of his clothing and searched. Naked, he had to shower and wash while guards watched. He was given prison clothing and led to a door of bars. A buzzer sounded, and the door slid open. Guy Paul walked through and the door clanged shut behind him, the sound of metal on metal echoed and bounced in Guy Paul's head. That sound would haunt his dreams for the rest of his life.

It was a fact that anyone convicted of a crime against children didn't do very well in prison. They were usually assaulted by the other prisoners, sometimes even killed. Most of the time, convicted child molesters and killers were kept separate from the other prisoners for their safety. Guy Paul begged to be kept away from everyone else. He knew his life was in danger. Prison officials refused and threw him into a cell right in the middle of all the other criminals. There was no protection for him. A twenty-five-year sentence: how would he survive?

"It was scarier than ever," Guy Paul said about the day he was taken to prison. "You could hear a pin drop even with the television on in the corner. Everyone was standing along the rails. I didn't know what was going to happen when they shut that door behind me. [Were] they going to kill me . . . or what?"

Guy Paul was living a nightmare. Not only was he innocent and locked away in prison, he was attacked and sexually assaulted by fellow inmates. He felt trapped, and lived in fear. He didn't know it then, but help was on its way.

Win Wahrer, now Director of Client Services of AIDWYC (Association in the Defence of the Wrongly Convicted), followed the case of Guy Paul Morin in the newspapers, and was not convinced he was guilty.

"I never met Guy Paul Morin until his bail hearing," she says. "I met with Peter Meier and other concerned citizens who all believed that Guy Paul Morin was innocent. I wrote a letter to Jack Pinkofsky and the Morin family through Mr. Pinkofsky's office. That is how this all started.

"Mrs. Morin called me to thank me [for the letter] and then I spoke to her daughter, Diane, who asked to meet with me. And that is when I was advised that there were two people who were trying to draft a petition and I was asked to meet with them, which I did. And that is when the Justice for Guy Paul Morin Committee was formed. Our job, as we saw it, was to educate the public at large concerning Guy Paul Morin's case. Part of what we did was to circulate a petition, write letters, and garner the support of politicians and the public at large. We did a fax blitz, held a vigil, and garnered the support of people like Joyce Milgaard, Rubin Hurricane Carter."

Ida Morin, desperate to save her son, contacted the committee and asked for help. They suggested lawyer James Lockyer.

On Guy Paul's behalf, Lockyer launched an *appeal* of the conviction to the Court of Appeal for Ontario on August 22, 1992, based on 181 legal grounds. His appeal questioned both the reliability of the evidence at the first and second trial, and questioned the significance of the hair-and-fibre evidence.

Lockyer also applied for bail for his client. But Guy Paul Morin was a convicted murderer of a nine-year-old girl. Bail was a long shot, at best.

After listening to the evidence presented by Lockyer,

Justice Marvin Catzman granted the bail.

"I would have to be mad if I didn't see something wrong with this case," he said.

The court set bail at $40,000 and Guy Paul was released on February 9, 1993, to await the findings of the appeal. He had served eighteen months in prison.

When bail was granted, the Morins celebrated. Finally, someone was listening and there was hope. Guy Paul was thrilled. He knew he was innocent and he knew the *DNA* tests they were asking for in the appeal would prove it. He celebrated his freedom with ice skating, dinners out with his now-fiancée Fiona, music, and his family.

The Jessops were devastated. Their little girl had been brutally murdered and the man they were told — were convinced — had killed her was now free on bail. They were stunned, furious, mortified.

"I hope he is enjoying himself," said Janet Jessop. "It's wonderful that he can go out for supper and go skating; Christine certainly can't and she will never be able to."

"I feel he's dancing on her grave. He's flaunting it."

"This is a fact." Morin told *The Globe and Mail.* "The final word will be . . . when my conviction is overturned and an *acquittal* entered."

17

CHAPTER SEVENTEEN

THE TRUTH AT LAST

JANUARY 23, 1995

Finally, people were working to prove Guy Paul was innocent instead of trying to make him look guilty.

In October 1994, the Chief Justice of Ontario ordered three scientists to jointly examine all of the available semen samples from the case and try to do a DNA profile.

The semen found on Christine's underpants was tested using new DNA testing that hadn't been available during the first two trials. The underpants were weathered and in poor condition, and the first two DNA tests were unsuccessful. On January 19, 1995, by using new techniques, the scientists finally produced a clear genetic profile of the killer. By comparing these results with Morin's DNA, it was concluded that the DNA from the sperm sample did not match Guy Paul Morin. Guy Paul

Morin was proven innocent of the rape and murder of Christine Jessop.

James Lockyer, Morin's lawyer, shared the good news about the DNA findings with Guy Paul. The findings were submitted to the Court of Appeal as fresh evidence.

"The evidence proves as an indisputable scientific fact that Mr. Morin is not guilty of the first-degree murder of Christine Jessop, and should be acquitted," said Crown counsel Kenneth L. Campbell in his address to the court at the appeal.

Guy Paul's acquittal, based purely on the new DNA evidence, came on January 23, 1995, by a *directed verdict* — a judgement made solely by the judge, without a trial or jury. Guy Paul Morin was in the courtroom to hear the best news of his life: *Innocent of the crime, and all charges dropped!*

He left the courthouse a free man for the first time in ten years.

"I've known I was innocent for the past ten years and finally, DNA has proven it scientifically, thank God," he told the crowd of reporters on the steps of the courthouse.

"I think there are a lot of people out there who made major mistakes," Morin says. "Were they deliberate? I don't know. There should be an inquiry to determine whether they should be charged."

There was an investigation of the police officers and the scientists involved in this case. While the investigation took place, the individuals remained on active duty and never suffered any consequences.

The general public has many theories on how and why an innocent man was framed for this crime. They can be read online at a number of different blogs and chat rooms. Even though these are only the speculations of a frustrated public, their questions and opinions are valid and include the following: Why did the police, scientists, and Crown have such tunnel vision? Were they simply frustrated with a difficult case full of mistakes that needed covering up? Were some of those "mistakes" made on purpose in order to hide the identity of the real killer and let him walk free? We may never know the answers to these questions, or find the real killer, because so much evidence was destroyed or tampered with.

"It all comes down to feeling like you've been lied to for ten years," said Kenny Jessop.

One of the key questions throughout the case of Guy Paul Morin is: How much did the town's perception of Guy Paul play in the conviction of an innocent man? Guy Paul Morin was mentioned a number of times by his neighbours, as well as by police, as being "odd" or "weird." So much so that his defence addressed those perceptions in the first trial, and they were again brought to the forefront in the second trial. Some criticism was made in regards to the back-up plea of insanity. Would Guy Paul have been found guilty in the first trial if the insanity plea hadn't been introduced? If it hadn't been thrown out in the second trial, perhaps he would have been found not guilty again.

Ida Morin told a reporter from *The New York Times*, "I myself knew and my husband knew that he was innocent. We could account for him, and twice we've written to that effect, once at the first trial and once at the second. It is a terrible thing not to be believed. The truth was not enough, and that's unfortunate."

"Christine and I shared a birthday, November 29. It's sad she never had a chance to share it with me," said Ida. "Christine's family suffered the loss of a dear daughter and for a decade the Morin family suffered the loss and wrongful conviction of a son and brother."

18

CHAPTER EIGHTEEN

THE KAUFMAN COMMISSION

FEBRUARY 10, 1997

On June 26, 1996, the Lieutenant Governor in Council ordered a Public Inquiry into the wrongful conviction of Guy Paul Morin. The Honourable Fred Kaufman, a former judge of the Quebec Court of Appeal, was appointed commissioner under the designation "The Commission of Proceedings Involving Guy Paul Morin."

Announcing the formation of the commission, Attorney General Charles Harnick said, "An inquiry cannot wipe away the years of pain and turmoil Mr. Morin suffered, but it can examine the complex circumstances surrounding the case, and allow us to learn from it and prevent any future miscarriage of justice."

Public hearings began on February 10, 1997, and continued for 146 days, ending on December 18, 1997. The Commission's three main roles were:

- *Investigative:* Why did the investigation into the death of Christine Jessop and the proceedings which followed result in the arrest and conviction of an innocent person?
- *Educational:* It was hoped that a public inquiry might help members of the community understand more about how the criminal justice system works and how the system worked in the case against Guy Paul Morin in particular.
- *Advisory:* The main focus of the Inquiry was to recommend changes that could prevent a future miscarriage of justice.

There were seven phases of the inquiry's public hearings. Two of them looked at the investigations of the York and Durham Regional Police Services. One focused on the issues arising from the two trials. The others were: Jail House Informant Testimony; Forensic Evidence; the Ontario Centre of Forensic Sciences; and Systemic Issues (basic things that are wrong with the way the justice system works).

A total of 120 witnesses were called to testify in front of the Inquiry. The Commissioner went through the transcripts of evidence and exhibits from both trials as well as the appeal documents. It amounted to more than 100,000 pages.

Ken and Janet Jessop told the Inquiry they had lied about their arrival time at the second trial. They told the Inquiry they had in fact arrived home at 4:10 p.m. They also stated that the police had pressured them and convinced them that their neighbour, Guy Paul Morin, was a "demon" and they had evidence that he had killed before. If they didn't change their arrival time, they were told the killer, Guy Paul Morin, would go free and probably kill again.

Another disturbing fact was discovered during the inquiry. Fibres relating to the Morin case had been contaminated while they were in the possession of the CFS. Red animal hairs were found on fibre tapes taken from the victim's clothing and the contents of the vacuum bag from Morin's Honda. These placed Christine in the vehicle. But it turned out that the assistant who processed the clothing at CFS was wearing a red angora sweater and not wearing a lab coat. The contamination was not reported to either the Crown or the defence.

At the Inquiry, Lockyer asked the head of the hair-and-fibre department of the CFS about hiding or suppressing the contamination during the trials.

"I don't know about suppressing it," the man responded. "I just didn't make it available."

"Interesting linguistics," Lockyer said. "So the two of

you testified at the 1992 trial while knowing this?"

"It would appear so," he admitted.

In addition to the red fibre contamination, the tapings from the seat covers and carpeting of the Morins' Honda were removed from the Christine Jessop evidence bag and thrown away. The authorities believed Guy Paul Morin was the murderer; therefore anything that did not connect him to the killing was destroyed, thrown out, or simply ignored.

Stephanie Nyznyk, forensic scientist, told the commission that she may have let the police and Crown believe the hair-and-fibre evidence was more important than it was, and they, in turn, misled the court. In other words, she had reported that the hair in Christine's necklace was a match to Guy Paul's. In fact, the hairs were similar but there was no proof that they were a match.

May, one of the jailhouse informants, told people after the trial he had lied about Guy Paul Morin confessing. He later tried to say he lied about lying.

Mr. X told the Inquiry that "at times I apparently lost contact with reality. I heard voices in my head which, sometimes, were so loud that I thought my head was going to explode." The Commission found that "Mr. X is an untrustworthy person whose testimony cannot be accepted on any of the issues before the Inquiry." The

Inquiry also found out that the prosecution had done favours for the two jailhouse informants.

Kaufman made 119 recommendations in all, including limits on what can be promised to convicted prisoners in exchange for evidence against someone else.

The most important recommendations related to helping stop police and prosecutors from developing tunnel vision. These include better interviewing techniques, rules about gathering and storing evidence, and ongoing education to keep professionals up-to-date on ways to improve their investigations.

Questions were raised regarding the dropping of certain suspects. Polygraph tests were used as an investigative tool on suspects. On the advice from lawyers, not all suspects agreed to take a polygraph. Once a suspect was cleared by a polygraph exam, it seemed he or she was dropped as a suspect. Guy Paul Morin had refused to take a polygraph. Prosecutor Gover told the Inquiry that: "I think clearly the investigators came to the view that the other suspects were cleared simply on the basis of their growing feeling that Mr. Morin was the perpetrator of these acts."

While Guy Paul Morin's pivotal legal point was his acquittal of this crime, his life-changing point was when Kenny Jessop, Christine's brother, was on the witness stand during the Kaufman Inquiry. While staring at the man he had once completely believed killed his sister, Kenny apologized, emotionally stating (regarding lying about their arrival time at home):

"Frankly, I don't give a damn if I'm charged. I want the truth to come out. I'm sorry, Paul. We thought we were doing the right thing, what the police told us to do. I'm telling the truth for the record so the truth can come out of all this."

The climax to the inquiry was this statement:

> On July 30, 1992, an innocent person was convicted of a heinous crime. The man was Guy Paul Morin and the crime was the first-degree murder of nine-year-old Christine Jessop, abducted from Queensville, Ontario, on October 3, 1984. It was not until January 23, 1995, almost ten years after he was first arrested, that Guy Paul Morin was exonerated as a result of the sophisticated DNA testing not previously available.
>
> The criminal proceedings against Guy Paul Morin represent a tragedy not only for Mr. Morin and his family, but also for the commun-

ity at large: the system failed him, a system for which we, the community, must bear responsibility. An innocent man was arrested, stigmatized, imprisoned, and convicted. The real killer has never been found. The trail grows colder with each passing year. For Christine Jessop's family there is no closure.

The reasons for the failure are set out in the pages which follow, and so are suggestions for change, designed to make similar failures less likely.

The report's findings include: faulty work by scientists at the CFS in Toronto, the questionable use of jailhouse informants, faking and misplacing evidence, and more.

Recommendation 32 was for the Jessops. Kaufman called for the establishment of a national DNA data bank; it became a reality on July 5, 2000. Now, all convicted criminals have their DNA put into the data bank. When a crime is committed and DNA evidence is available from the crime scene, it is compared with what's in the data bank to see if there is a match.

At the end, the report found that Guy Paul Morin was innocent of the crime beyond the shadow of a doubt. Kaufman also stated that he believed that no one tried to convict an innocent man on purpose. "Rather," he said, "they developed a staggering tunnel vision" and it was that tunnel vision which led to serious mistakes in judgement. Not only did the tunnel vision wrongly convict an innocent man, it also let the real murderer of Christine Jessop escape.

"Science helped to convict him, science exonerated him. We will never know if Guy Paul Morin would have been exonerated had DNA testing not been available."

Kaufman turned to Guy Paul Morin and said: "Though this was not one of the stated purposes of the Inquiry, I am pleased that it has served to explain and demonstrate your innocence."

Christine Jessop's murder is still unsolved.

James Treleaven, Q.C., gave evidence at the Inquiry and stated: "My suspicion is that . . . some people at the start of this Inquiry still harboured lingering doubts about Mr. Morin, and I think that one of the useful functions this Commission has served is to make it clear. I mean, nobody could sit, as I have, through day after day of this evidence . . . without saying: How can there be any doubt?"

Ms. MacLean broke down in tears and apologized for having cast doubt on Mr. Morin's exoneration and acquittal. "I'm not proud of having been involved in the prosecution of someone who is innocent," she testified at the Inquiry. "I've lost sleep over it. I'm still trying to grasp it."

"This closes a chapter, a big chapter, in my life," said Guy Paul later in an interview. "We all have our own genetic pattern and isn't that wonderful. And it is wonderful for you as much as it is for me. Because what happened to me could happen to you, and I have been through an experience that I would not wish on anyone."

EPILOGUE: WHAT NOW?

After the recommendations from the Inquiry were released, Dr. James Young, Ontario's chief coroner, stated that changes were already in the works including the installation of a state-of-the-art hair-and-fibre analysis lab costing more than $750,000.

During the Kaufman Commission, selected members of the Metropolitan Toronto Police (now the Toronto Police Service) formed the Jessop Task Force in 1995 to reopen the case in hopes of finding the killer. The nine-man group, headed by Detective Sergeant Neale Tweedy, led what he termed an "aggressive, ongoing investigation." They had a huge mess to wade through which included over 360 suspects. Besides the challenge of the passing of years, there was missing evidence, and witnesses and people who had called in tips had moved or were untraceable. The two police forces, Durham and

York, had different filing systems and note-taking procedures, as well as rules governing the destruction of those documents. The team tried to match DNA from the semen stain to their list of suspects. They even tested Ken. Nobody was a match. Then they tested the DNA at the crime scene against 27,000 persons by using the new DNA data bank. No match was found. The task force disbanded without solving the case.

Twenty-seven years have passed since the abduction and murder of nine-year-old Christine Jessop. However, Detective Keith Bradshaw, of the Cold Case/Special Investigation section of the Toronto Police Service Homicide Squad, states: "There are no closed murder cases. If any new leads or information are brought to light, they will be investigated. This is a case that is just waiting to be solved."

Guy Paul Morin received a full apology from the Ontario Attorney General Charles Harnick and a $1.25 million settlement payable to him and his parents. But it came at a great personal cost for Guy Paul. Not only had he lost years, it cost him his relationship with his girlfriend, Fiona. However, Guy Paul bounced back and started seeing a wonderful girl named Allison Ferguson. They were married in March of 1995 in the Virgin Islands. After they returned home from a honeymoon cruise, Guy Paul cut a CD of clarinet music and had plans to work as a repairman with his own company, "Paul's Handiworks Ltd." Last reported, Al and Ida have moved from Queensville and Guy Paul and Allison are now living west of Toronto with their children.

The quaint hamlet of Queensville, perched on the top of a rolling Ontario hill, gives the impression that this is a good and safe place to raise a family. The elementary school looks unchanged over the years, except for a few outbuildings and a red oak planted in memory of Christine Jessop. From the parking area in front of the corner store, you can still see the Jessops' old driveway on the top of the next rise. The house, ironically, had been a funeral home before the Jessops owned it and is now a Montessori school. An old wooden fence separates the old Jessop house from the neighbour's, just as it did when the Morins lived next door. And behind this house is the Queensville Cemetery where Christine used to love to play, where now, about a hundred metres away, she lies for eternity. While little has changed in Queensville, the memory of the unsolved murder, and the wrongful conviction of one of their own, is still alive in those who live there.

AUTHOR'S NOTE

The wrongful conviction of Guy Paul Morin brought national attention to some of the flaws in the Canadian legal system, as noted in the Kaufman Commission, which can be found at www.ontla.on.ca/library/repository/mon/10000/201163.pdf. Some of the changes have been huge. For example, DNA testing has been expanded and advanced in technology since this case came to light. Canada's DNA data bank can now compare and match DNA from known criminals and link them to previous crimes. It is now used to rule out suspects. If it had been in place before Guy Paul had been arrested, he most likely would never have been charged in the first place.

This case also led to changes in police procedures in criminal cases. The use of jailhouse informants, how police record and store evidence, conduct interviews, and maintain their notes have all been improved. It's not perfect, but the justice system has moved forward based on the findings of the Kaufman Commission.

Guy Paul Morin was supported after his conviction in 1992 by a unique organization — The Justice for Guy Paul Morin Committee. Later, this group founded the Association in Defence of the Wrongly Convicted (AIDWYC). They have been responsible for overturning the wrongful convictions of a number of Canadians and continue to fight on their behalf. This group alone has forced the justice system to see many basic problems within the system and address them. For more information, please visit their website at www.aidwyc.org.

ACKNOWLEDGEMENTS

A HUGE thank you to Kirk Makin, Justice Reporter for *The Globe and Mail* and author of the national bestseller *Redrum the Innocent* for writing the foreword to this book, and granting permission for the use of some of his photos. You have patiently answered my emails and offered your help so graciously. You are a consummate professional.

A special thanks to Detective Keith Bradshaw, of the Cold Case/Special Investigation section of the Toronto Police Service Homicide Squad, whose information and direction was very helpful, as well as Detective Jim Van Allen with the Behavioural Science section of the Ontario Provincial Police. Thanks also for all the help received from the scientists and staff at the Centre for Forensic Science in Ontario. I would like to acknowledge John Lattimore-Durant, Child Find Ontario Executive Director, for providing me with statistical information. A big thank you to Peter Wiinholt, Kenny Jessop's grade-six teacher, and Jeff from the Queensville cemetery. Author Rick Mofina, thank you for graciously responding to my emails and questions.

Pam Hickman, a special thank you to you and the staff at Formac and Lorimer. You are all talented, patient, and wonderful to work with.

I would be remiss if I didn't mention AIDWYC, and specifically Win Wahrer, who has spent much time and energy answering my questions and lending her support. Thank you, Win, and all of you at AIDWYC who work so diligently to right the wrongs made by Canada's justice system.

TIMELINE

1983: The Jessop family moves to Queensville from Richmond Hill, Ontario

OCTOBER 3, 1984: Christine Jessop goes missing

DECEMBER 31, 1984: Christine Jessop's body is found near the town of Sunderland in Durham Region, 56 kilometres east of Queensville, Ontario

JANUARY 2, 1985: The Jessop autopsy is performed by Dr. John Hillsdon-Smith, chief pathologist at the coroner's office

JANUARY 7, 1985: The body of Christine Jessop is buried in the Queensville cemetery, behind her family's home

FEBRUARY 20, 1985: Shephard identifies Guy Paul Morin as "Suspect Morin" in his notebook

FEBRUARY 22, 1985: Police first question next-door neighbour, Guy Paul Morin

APRIL 22, 1985: Guy Paul Morin is arrested for the rape and first-degree murder of Christine Jessop

OCTOBER 7, 1985: Mr. Justice John Osler grants a defence application for an order changing the venue for the trial, directing that it take place in London, Ontario, due to the extensive media coverage

JANUARY 7, 1986: The first trial of Guy Paul Morin begins in London, Ontario

FEBRUARY 7, 1986: Guy Paul Morin is acquitted after thirteen hours of deliberation

MARCH 4, 1986: The Ontario Attorney General files notice in the Ontario Court of Appeal alleging two errors fatal to the acquittal

JUNE 5, 1987: A new trial is ordered by the Court of Appeal for Ontario and Morin is arrested a few days later

JUNE 7, 1987: An attempt to reinstate the death penalty in Canada results in parliamentary debates and a vote to confirm the status quo

NOVEMBER 17, 1988: Morin appeals to the Supreme Court of Canada in regards to being re-charged.

MAY 28, 1990: Morin's second preliminary inquiry begins

OCTOBER 30, 1990: Christine Jessop's body is exhumed at the request of defence lawyer Jack Pinkofsky

NOVEMBER 4, 1990: Christine's remains are reburied in the Queensville cemetery

NOVEMBER 13, 1991: Opening statements of the second trial

JULY 30, 1992: Guy Paul Morin is found guilty of the first-degree rape and murder of nine-year-old

Christine Jessop after the nine-month trial

AUGUST 22, 1992: Guy Paul Morin launches appeal

FEBRUARY 1993: Guy Paul Morin is granted bail of $120,000, pending his appeal by Justice Marvin Catzman

JANUARY 23, 1995: Guy Paul Morin is exonerated on the strength of DNA evidence after eighteen months in prison and ten years of being accused of the murder of Christine Jessop

JUNE 26, 1996: The Lieutenant Governor in Council directs that a Public Inquiry be held and the Honourable Fred Kaufman, Q.C., a former judge of the Quebec Court of Appeal, is named as commissioner over the proceedings

FEBRUARY 10, 1997: Public hearings begin and continue for 146 days

APRIL 9, 1998: Release of the Report of the Kaufman Commission on Proceedings Involving Guy Paul Morin

1998: A three-year task force investigating the killing is disbanded

GLOSSARY

ACQUITTAL: the verdict when someone accused of a crime is found not guilty.

ALIBI: a defence in which the defendant attempts to prove that he or she was in another place when the crime was committed.

AMBER ALERT: a media alert issued when it is suspected that a child has been abducted.

APPEAL: a request to review a case that has already been decided in court.

CONVICTION: the verdict when someone accused of a crime is found guilty.

CROWN ATTORNEY: the lawyer(s) acting for the government, or "the Crown," in court proceedings. They are the prosecutors in Canada's legal system.

DEFENDANT: the person who has been formally accused of and charged with committing a crime.

DIRECTED VERDICT: the verdict when the judge finds the prosecution has failed to prove their case. After a directed verdict, there is no longer any need for the jury to decide the case. A directed verdict in a criminal case is an acquittal for the defendant.

DNA: (Deoxyribonucleic acid) is a microscopic, double-stranded element in the cells of the body. It is unique to each individual, except for identical twins. In the legal system it's been hailed as the greatest advance in investigations since the fingerprint. A fleck of skin, a strand of hair, blood, or other body fluids found at a crime scene can provide a sample of DNA. The sample can be compared to one taken from an accused person to see if they match. A DNA profile takes up to three months of lab work to produce.

EXPERT TESTIMONY: Expert evidence must be based in science, not in guessing or opinion. This rule made DNA acceptable evidence in Canada, and led to the freeing of wrongly convicted people such as David Milgaard and Guy Paul Morin.

FORENSICS: the study of medical facts in relation to legal cases.

FIRST-DEGREE MURDER: the planned or deliberate killing of another human being. In Canada, there are thirteen conditions under which someone can be charged with first-degree murder. Murder while committing or attempting to commit aggravated sexual assault is one of them.

JURY: A criminal trial is decided by a group of twelve randomly selected citizens from the province in which the trial is held. All twelve must agree on a verdict.

MOTIONS: a request to the judge to make a decision regarding a contested issue in the case. Motions may be made at any point during a trial.

PERJURY: intentionally lying while on the stand.

PROFILING: a tool intended to help investigators identify an unknown criminal through listing probable social and psychological traits of the offender based on the known facts of the case.

PROSECUTOR: the lawyer acting for the prosecution, usually the state (in Canada, the Crown). The prosecutor tries to prove the defendant is guilty.

SIMPLE SCHIZOPHRENIA: a disorder in which a person shows some of the symptoms of schizophrenia without experiencing psychotic episodes; for example, sudden withdrawal from social and work situations.

TESTIMONY: the statement of a witness under oath.

VERDICT: the decision of the jury at the end of a trial, usually guilty or not guilty.

FURTHER READING

ONLINE

For the reader who wishes to find out more about this fascinating case, a rich resource of documents and news articles is available online through the following link:
http://www.cbc.ca/archives/categories/society/crime-
    justice/cold-cases-unsolved-crimes-in-canada/
    christine-jessop-queensville-ont-1984.html

This website link is a blog which contains an interesting conversation by Christine Jessop's brother, Ken Jessop:
http://www.unsolvedcanada.ca/index.php?topic=
    2085.0

INTERMEDIATE RESOURCES

Makin, Kirk. *Redrum the Innocent.* Toronto: Penguin, 1992.
The Commission on Proceedings Involving Guy Paul Morin, the Honourable Fred Kaufman, C.M., Q.C. by Order in Council, June 26, 1996.
Sampirisi, Jenny. "Like Bone From Skin." (Thesis, University of Windsor, 2006)

NEWSPAPER AND MAGAZINE ARTICLES

The Brandon Sun article by Mark Dunn (1995)

The Era Banner article by Martin Derbyshire (2004)

The Globe and Mail articles by Kirk Makin (1995, 2004)

The Lethbridge Herald articles by Canadian Press (1987, 1990, 1992)

Maclean's articles by Patricia Chisholm with Sharon Doyle Driedger ("Morin Freed by DNA," February 6, 1995), Tom Fennell with Danylo Hawaleshka ("Morin Inquiry Revelations," July 1, 1997)

New York Times article by Clyde H. Farnsworth (1995)

Toronto Star articles by Peter Cheney (1986), Tracey Tyler (2007)

Winnipeg Free Press articles by Canadian Press (1986, 1988), Wendy Cox (1992, 1995), Gloria Galloway (1996), Paul Atab (1997)

PHOTO CREDITS

We gratefully acknowledge the following sources for permission to reproduce the images contained within this book:

Al Dunlop/The Canadian Press: front cover, p. 43

Cynthia J. Faryon: back cover (three on right)

Ken Faught/The Canadian Press: p. 46

Kirk Makin. *Redrum The Innocent*. Toronto: Viking Canada, 1992: back cover (left), p. 44, 45

INDEX